Agendas for
Second Language Literacy

CAMBRIDGE LANGUAGE EDUCATION
Series Editor: Jack C. Richards

An authoritative series drawing on the best available research and practice to present effective approaches to language teaching.

In this series:

Agendas for Second Language Literacy *by Sandra Lee McKay*

Reflective Teaching in Second Language Classrooms
by Jack C. Richards and Charles Lockhart

An Integrative Approach to Educating Second Language Children *edited by Fred Genesee*

Agendas for
Second Language Literacy

Sandra Lee McKay

San Francisco State University

CAMBRIDGE
UNIVERSITY PRESS

Published by the Press Syndicate of the University of Cambridge
The Pitt Building, Trumpington Street, Cambridge CB2 1RP
40 West 20th Street, New York, NY 10011-4211, USA
10 Stamford Road, Oakleigh, Melbourne 3166, Australia

© Cambridge University Press 1993

First published 1993

Printed in the United States of America

Library of Congress Cataloging-in-Publication Data

McKay, Sandra.
Agendas for second language literacy / Sandra Lee McKay.
p.   cm. – (Cambridge language education)
Includes bibliographical references and index.
ISBN 0-521-44118-8 (hardback). – ISBN 0-521-44664-3 (pbk.)
1. Second language acquisition.   2. Literacy.   I. Title.
II. Series.
P118.2.M34   1993
306.4'49 – dc20
                                                                92-40939
                                                                    CIP

A catalog record for this book is available from the British Library

ISBN 0-521-44118-8 hardback
ISBN 0-521-44664-3 paperback

To my husband, for his support and advice

Contents

Foreword

Agendas for Second Language Literacy is not only about literacy, it is about people – people who have their own purposes and hopes for learning literacy in English. The discussion in these pages about definitions, policies, and practices is woven together with tales of human activity and accounts of individuals making sense of the world. In this way, Sandra McKay illuminates the consequences of these definitions, policies, and practices for human lives.

The author invites us to examine with her the contexts that shape what happens in the second language literacy classroom. Beginning with a wide lens of national policy, then narrowing our focus to the economic arena, the family, and the classroom, McKay helps us to see more clearly the forces that shape our work and determine its efficacy. There are three layers of lenses that McKay leads us through before we get to the classroom, where our own work is enacted, making it clear that the issues are large and complex and that our teaching may be a very small piece of the picture.

Although it is humbling to know our limits, it enables us to know the possibilities that we can support through our work. McKay invites us to give thought to the ways we teach and to the ways that we, as teachers, may act as mediators, negotiating the link between the policies driving our programs and the possibilities for meeting the agendas of our students in the context of their daily lives. By understanding both the possibilities and the limits, I believe we may have a better hope for making a difference.

In *Agendas for Second Language Literacy,* McKay provides information, but she also challenges us. How much do we know about the policies that determine who our students will be? How much do we know about the policies that drive the funding of our programs and how this influences the content and materials we teach? How much do we know about the home situations of the students we serve and the purposes these adults have for being in our classrooms?

I believe that it behooves us to find out. We can't do it alone – it must be a collective effort. *Agendas for Second Language Literacy* is an excellent way to start the conversation.

Gail Weinstein-Shr

Series Editor's Preface

The Cambridge Language Education Series draws on the best available research, theory, and educational practice to help clarify issues and resolve problems in language teaching, language teacher education, and related areas. Books in the series focus on a wide range of issues and are written in a style that is accessible to classroom teachers, teachers-in-training, and teacher educators.

In *Agendas for Second Language Literacy,* Sandra McKay describes the many ways in which literacy issues affect the lives of second language learners, both within and outside the family. By surveying a broad range of cases from North America, Australia, and the United Kingdom, Professor McKay convincingly illustrates the kinds of literacy-related issues that have emerged as a consequence of large-scale immigration. Among these issues are the status of the mother tongue, language policy, language education provision, and employment needs. Each chapter examines a different agenda – including the sociopolitical, economic, familial, and educational – with discussions ranging from the linguistic to the psycholinguistic, cognitive, cultural, economic, and political aspects of attaining literacy in a new language. At the same time, the depth of information presented serves as a useful basis for facilitating decisions about literacy policies and for determining appropriate goals, contents, and procedures in literacy education.

Agendas for Second Langauge Literacy is an invaluable resource for anyone involved in making provisions for the development of literacy in a second language.

Jack C. Richards

Preface

As social, economic, and political circumstances create the conditions for immigration to English-speaking countries, a large number of speakers of other languages are striving to become literate in English. There is a growing literature dealing with various aspects of English literacy for native English speakers in which the plurality of "literacies" is examined. However, there are few books available that specifically address the nature of second language literacy or that examine the sociopolitical, economic, familial, and educational contexts in which language minorities attempt to become literate in English.

Current literature on literacy rightly suggests that the classroom is only one of several forces affecting individual literacy. The family, the educational system, the sociopolitical milieu all have agendas for literacy, with associated assumptions about who should acquire literacy, how they should acquire it, in what language, and for what purpose. At times these agendas conflict with one another with the result that, for example, a stated sociopolitical agenda for universal literacy may conflict with an economic agenda for limited literacy that ensures a supply of unskilled labor. At other times an individual or community agenda for literacy in a language other than English may conflict with an educational or sociopolitical agenda for literacy in English only. This book will explore such conflicting agendas for literacy, with attention to the relevancy of these conflicts for the individual and for the second language classroom.

Agendas for Second Language Literacy is organized into six chapters according to the common arenas that can influence agendas for literacy, namely the sociopolitical, economic, familial, and educational contexts. Each chapter examines the following questions:

1. What assumptions about literacy are promoted within the particular context?
2. What specific policies, traditions, or actions establish second language literacy agendas within each context?

3. How do these agendas affect an individual's endeavor to become literate in a second language?

Drawing on case studies of various families, countries, and literacy programs, the chapters examine literacy agendas affecting language minorities in Anglophone countries. Case studies are included throughout the book for two reasons. First, the case studies demonstrate the special complexities of second language literacy in which the assumptions regarding literacy specified by an individual's home culture may conflict with those of the second culture. Second, they permit a comparative as well as a culture-specific view of literacy, allowing greater breadth in the book's discussion of second language literacy.

In *Agendas for Second Language Literacy, literacy* is viewed as a multidimensional construct in which the meaning of literacy depends on who is defining the term. Actors within specific contexts define literacy to meet their own agendas; for example, an employer may describe literacy in terms of efficiency in job-related tasks, whereas an employee may be concerned with literacy for job mobility. An educational administrator may define success in literacy in terms of scores on discrete item tests; however, success for language minorities may rest on their ability to read to their children. The contradictions between contexts are problematic when the requirements for literacy in one situation are considered inadequate in another.

Throughout the book, the value of literacy in languages other than English is emphasized. Thus, when literacy is used in the book it is not meant to be equated with English literacy. When it is necessary to distinguish literacy in a particular language, the term itself is prefaced with a specific language. The term *language minorities* refers to individuals who are permanent residents of Anglophone countries and who speak a language other than English in their home. These individuals can be immigrants, refugees, or citizens, but not sojourners.

Agendas for Second Language Literacy is addressed to teachers of nonnative speakers of English, whether they be mainstream, English as a second language, or bilingual education teachers. It is also addressed to individuals involved in developing second language literacy policies in the political, labor, and educational sectors. The ultimate goal of the book is to provide these individuals with an understanding of the manner in which the literacy agendas of the larger sociopolitical, economic, and familial contexts affect second language learners, thus encouraging educators and policymakers to consider carefully the kinds of literacy agendas they wish to support. In order to accomplish this goal, the book focuses to a large extent on issues of policy. It does so in the belief that an awareness of such issues enables educators and others involved in second language education to design and assess literacy programs and curricula, not only on the basis of their pedagogical soundness but also in light of their social, cultural, and political ramifications.

The book begins with an examination of the concept of literacy. In Chapter 1, "The Plurality of Literacies," various definitions and perspectives of literacy are examined and related specifically to second language literacy. It points out how, in many Anglophone countries, literacy is frequently defined only in reference to English literacy with little value attached to mother-tongue literacy. The chapter also illustrates the conflicts that biliterate individuals can encounter in acquiring second language literacy owing to cultural differences in discourse style, social labels attached to various literacy levels, and a lack of shared literacy goals.

Chapter 2 explores the way in which the sociopolitical context sets second language literacy agenda through such issues as national language policies, immigration and naturalization requirements, literacy campaigns, and the designation of a medium of instruction for public schools. The chapter argues that, in many instances, such policies restrict the linguistic choices available to second language learners. Although at times these policies are made in response to economic and feasibility issues rather than lack of support for biliteracy, their impact nevertheless is generally to severely limit the ability of language minorities to develop mother-tongue literacy.

Chapter 3 focuses on the relationship between literacy and economic rewards. This chapter demonstrates that political and business leaders as well as workers often determine not only who will have the opportunity to develop English literacy but also who will benefit economically from this literacy. They accomplish this, for example, through government-sponsored job training programs, professional certification requirements, and union demands. Frequently, language minorities, owing in part to their lack of English literacy abilities, are not able to influence the design and enactment of such programs and policies in order to meet their own first and second language literacy goals. Throughout the chapter, English literacy is viewed as a necessary but by no means sufficient condition for economic success.

The relationship between literacy and the family is the focus of Chapter 4. The chapter discusses the ways in which families promote various literacy practices and in so doing create an environment for literacy learning. A major portion of the chapter is devoted to examining the manner in which researchers and educators set literacy agendas for families through their research methods and findings as well as through the implementation of family literacy programs. The chapter also examines the effect of English literacy on the dynamics of language minority families. It further discusses where the acquisition of English literacy ranks in reference to the overall needs of language minority families.

The fifth chapter discusses the way in which literacy program funders, curriculum designers, and teachers all set second language literacy agendas, at times resulting in the establishment of goals not necessarily shared by the learners themselves. The chapter describes various literacy programs and curricula and demonstrates that the manner in which such programs and curricula are judged depends to a large extent on the evaluator. Whereas funders or educators may rate a program quite highly, language minorities, depending on their literacy agendas, may not share the same evaluation. The chapter closes with a discussion of second language literacy assessment and argues for a participatory approach to literacy assessment.

The final chapter, "Agendas for Second Language Literacy," argues that, rather than approaching language minorities as a social and educational problem, political leaders and educators should focus on ways to aid language minorities in the attainment of their own English literacy goals. Such an approach, however, necessitates the willingness of all those involved in second language literacy to design and fund a great variety of literacy programs, always valuing first as well as second language literacy in the design and implementation of such programs.

A major assumption of the book is that all pedagogical programs and decisions reflect a set of social priorities, be they implicit or explicit. It is my belief that all those involved in second language literacy education – researchers, program funders and designers, materials writers, and teachers – should carefully consider what social priorities they wish to support in second language literacy education so that pedagogical decisions can be made with these priorities in mind. It is in the desire to contribute to such considerations that *Agendas for Second Language Literacy* was written.

This book would not have been possible without the help of both Gail Weinstein-Shr, who provided inspiration and direction for the scope of the book and constructive feedback in its development, and Heide Wrigley, who suggested valuable resources for the book and shared with me the many insights she gained from observing literacy programs throughout the United States. I am also grateful to Elsa Auerbach and James Tollefson for their careful reading and comments on the manuscript and to Jack Richards, Mary Vaughn, and Suzette André for their help throughout the publishing process.

1 The plurality of literacies

When Minh Tran, a Vietnamese refugee, decided to enroll in an adult
literacy class, he did so because he wanted to learn to read and write in
English so that he could resume his work as a medical technologist.
His wife, Hoa, was pleased with his decision, primarily because she
believed that if he were able to work as he had done in Vietnam, he
would be happier. She also hoped that once Minh learned to read and
write, he could tell her about news of Vietnam that appeared in the
English newspaper. Because the children, Mai and Hung, were young,
Hoa also knew that once they started school, they would need help
with English. However, she worried that as her husband and children
learned English, they might begin to forget their Vietnamese and that
she, knowing very little English, would become an outsider. Minh's
sister, Lan, hoped that once Minh learned to read and write, he could
help her make advertisements for the crafts she hoped to sell at local
fairs. Lan was acquiring a good deal of spoken English but had little
interest in learning to read and write. In fact, she had never acquired
literacy in her native language.

When Minh arrived at the local resettlement agency, he was referred
to a government-sponsored adult vocational literacy program. Once
there, he was assigned to a class that emphasized the functional literacy skills necessary to secure a job. The program was government
sponsored, funded with the goal of helping refugees become economically self-sufficient. Minh's teacher believed that students in the class
needed basic survival skills, which would allow them to fill out forms,
read bus schedules, and consult the local want-ad sections. Thus, he
tended to focus on survival literacy in his class.

Each individual in this scenario had his or her own agenda for
Minh's becoming literate. Each made assumptions about the ultimate
goal of Minh's literacy training, hoping to satisfy an often unstated
agenda. It is within these conflicting assumptions and goals that Minh,
like other language minorities, will begin learning to read and write in

1

English. In the process, the various agendas set by others may undermine his own goals. For Minh, who wants to become literate so that he can do the kind of work he did in Vietnam, reading about news of Vietnam, helping his sister with her business, or learning to read want ads in class may all seem unrelated to his goal. Yet as a husband, a brother, a student, he will have these goals set for him.

In this chapter we will examine the various meanings of literacy and suggest how these definitions frame what it means for Minh to become literate in English. To begin, we examine various definitions of literacy, focusing on how definitions of second language literacy/illiteracy have been constructed, with the understanding that such definitions always depend on who is defining the term and what their purpose is. Next, we explore the manner in which first language literacy can influence the acquisition of literacy in a second language. In the second part of the chapter, we discuss two prevalent perspectives of literacy: that of literacy as an individual accomplishment and that of literacy as a social practice. In dealing with literacy as an individual skill, we will consider how literacy has been defined in reference to achievement levels and how the development of literacy has been viewed as influencing cognitive development. In considering literacy as social practice, we will examine literacy from a historical, economic, political, and sociocultural perspective.

Definitions of literacy

The literacy/illiteracy construct

Illiteracy is a highly charged term, one that is often contrasted with *literacy,* as if individuals either are or are not literate. Such a dichotomy is a tremendous oversimplification. As Crandall (1992) notes:

> Dichotomies such as "literacy-illiteracy" or "functional literacy–functional illiteracy" are simplistic and reductionist, and the statistics of illiteracy which they engender, equally so. The complex notion of literacy cannot be captured by any one definition of skills, functions, or practices. This is especially true for language minority individuals, whose differential allocation of literacy across languages is complex. (p. 88)

In discussing literacy it is important to recognize that this dichotomy is an oversimplification. Furthermore, it is important to qualify literacy in reference to a particular language. For example, Minh is, in fact, already literate in Vietnamese. Should he then be considered as not literate in his new home?

In order to answer this question, it is helpful to consider the distinction made by Venezky (1990) regarding the relationship between English literacy and nonnative speakers of English in which he posits the following categories of speakers:

1. Nonnative speakers of English, literate in their own language.
2. Nonnative speakers of English, lacking required literacy in their own culture.
3. Nonspeakers of English, lacking required literacy in their own culture. (p. 13)

In this taxonomy, Minh belongs to category one, a category to which Venezky believes the term illiteracy should not apply unless qualified by not literate in English. Lan belongs to category two, a category to which Venezky believes the term illiterate should apply, but it is still important to distinguish between illiteracy in the native language and in English.

In terms of the third category, nonspeakers of English who are not literate in their native language, Venezky (1990) believes that the term illiterate might be used in reference to the individual's native language. However, he argues that the label has no import for such individuals in relation to English because everyone could then be labeled illiterate for every language they do not speak. As he puts it, illiterate "is not a functional label for those who neither read nor speak English, primarily because their illiteracy results automatically from their inability to speak English. Instruction in spoken English is a critical step in their acquisition of literacy" (p. 13). Viewed from this perspective, Hoa would not be labeled as illiterate in English because of her lack of familiarity with spoken English. Knowing a language, then, and becoming literate are two different things. For Venezky, a knowledge of spoken English is a prerequisite for being labeled literate or illiterate in English.

Although Venezky's categories are helpful in examining what it means to be not literate in English, these categories are not helpful in determining when one should be considered literate. One of the important problems that arises in trying to differentiate individuals who are considered literate from those who are not has to do with specifying what practices one must master to be considered literate. As we shall see shortly, many who study literacy posit various levels of abilities in dealing with the printed word. Is there a particular level one must attain to be considered literate by social standards? When Minh masters the alphabet in English and can read and write simple messages, should he be considered English literate, or must he attain additional abilities, and if so, what additional abilities?

A second problem that arises in distinguishing those who are literate from those who are not literate involves age level. It is unlikely that Minh's young children would be labeled illiterate in either their native language or English. At what age should the term illiteracy apply? In considering this question, Venezky points out that in reporting statistics on national literacy rates, literacy standards are frequently applied only to individuals above a certain age. This fact leads Venezky (1990) to conclude that literacy includes the idea of social relevancy. As he says, "if literacy is some complex of skills demonstrated in socially relevant contexts, then it is logical to assume that until one approaches adulthood there are not sufficient opportunities to apply these particular skills" (p. 5). Determining the abilities and practices that are necessary to be considered literate is a difficult task. Central to this task is an understanding of what it means to be literate. Such definitions, however, always depend on who is defining the term and what purpose they have.

All definitions of literacy include the idea that literacy entails the ability to deal with the written word. For many, however, literacy involves more than the ability to read and write a simple message. Some individuals accept the following definition of functional literacy adopted by UNESCO in 1962:

A person is literate when he has acquired the essential knowledge and skills which enable him to engage in all those activities in which literacy is required for effective functioning in his group and community, and whose attainment in reading, writing, and arithmetic make it possible for him to continue to use these skills towards his own and the community's development. (International Committee of Experts on Literacy Report, UNESCO, Paris, 1962, cited in Fingeret, 1982, pp. 63–64)

According to this definition, Minh will become functionally literate in English when he has sufficient reading and writing ability in English to fulfill his own personal objectives as well as meet the literacy demands made on him by society as a citizen, consumer, and worker. Some, however, reject the UNESCO definition, arguing that it frames literacy as a personal attribute rather than as a range of social practices.

Fisher (1978) contends that individuals who can cope within an environment in which print is required can be considered functionally literate whether or not they can pass reading and writing tests. Such individuals, he contends, are functionally literate in the sense that through oral means and an awareness of nonverbal cues, they can perform satisfactorily in a specific context. Venezky (1990), however, takes issue with this stance and argues that functional literacy requires "a defined set of skills as opposed to a coping behavior that might be based on deception, avoidance, or the literacy skills of others" (p. 7). Thus, according to Venezky, for Minh to be considered functionally English literate, he himself must be able to read and write to deal with his environment and not depend solely on other coping mechanisms such as seeking help from friends or using nonverbal cues in the environment to function in society.

What it means for Minh to function in society, however, will greatly depend on his own social network. As Mikulecky (1990) points out, "the purposes for which one uses literacy and the way one goes about using literacy to function often are related to how one functions in social networks" (p. 29). Landlords and school officials, for example, may require Minh to deal with printed material. If Minh is unable to deal with these things, he may ask help from friends who are more literate in English than he. On the other hand, Minh may use his English literacy to help his sister with her business. In this way, Minh's social network affects the way he uses literacy. Furthermore, his social network can affect his goals for literacy. His role in his family, for example, has likely been instrumental in his setting a goal to achieve the level of English literacy necessary for him to work as a medical technologist. Literacy then entails a range of practices and the social uses of these practices. Shortly, we will examine both of these aspects of literacy in depth. First, however, we will consider the relationship between native language literacy and second language literacy.

Acquiring second language literacy

In discussing bilingualism, Macias (1990a) delineates three kinds of literacy acquisition patterns: "native-language literacy, second-language literacy (implying no literacy in the native language for a bilingual), and biliteracy (literacy in two languages)" (p. 220). Throughout this book we will use *second language literacy* to refer to both second language literacy and biliteracy, in Macias's terms. However, this distinction is important to make when considering the process of acquiring literacy in a second language. Minh belongs to the last category and, as such, his literacy in his native language may be an asset in his acquiring English literacy. As Bell and Burnaby (1984) point out, adults who are already literate in their native language, particularly if it is an alphabetic language, have the following advantages:

They are trained in the visual discrimination of significant features in letter discrimination. They understand the concept of a particular sound being represented by a particular symbol. They have expectations of a certain content being presented in certain formats. Most important of all, they expect print to yield meaning. (p. 14)

A great deal of research suggests that there is a positive transfer of literacy skills learned in the first language to the second language (Canale, Frenette, & Belanger, 1988; Cummins, 1981, 1984; Hakuta, 1986). Weinstein (1984), for example, cites a study undertaken in a Thai refugee camp that investigated the effects of both prior formal education and literacy ability in another language on classroom performance in learning English. The study found that "literacy in any of the languages (Hmong, Laos, or Thai) produced a major effect on the subjects' performance on the ESL test: The ability to read helped the subjects in their efforts to learn another language" (Robson, 1981, as cited in Weinstein 1984, p. 473). Other studies, however, suggest that one may need to reach a certain level of proficiency in a second language for there to be a transfer effect (Alderson, 1984; Cummins, 1981) and that the transfer process is a complex phenomenon related to the individual's native language and the skill involved (Carson, Carrell, Silberstein, Kroll, & Kuehn, 1990).

Although a great deal of further research is needed to determine exactly how Minh's literacy in Vietnamese will affect his endeavor to become literate in English, there are two areas where some effect is likely. The first involves his use of one or the other language in specific domains. Minh may tend to read certain things in his first language and other things in his second language. Wallace (1988) contends that often the kind of reading and writing done in one's native language will "be undertaken in order to maintain feelings of identity with one's own community, ethnic group and family, where readers are taking on what we might call 'private' roles" (p. 6). On the other hand, the reading and writing that will occur in a second language "are more 'public' roles to do with being a member of the wider society, for example as motorist, consumer or taxpayer." To the degree this division occurs for Minh, he may become more proficient at reading and writing certain types of texts in his native language and certain types in English.

A second way in which Minh's literacy in his first language will likely affect his acquisition of second language literacy arises from the way discourse is organized in various languages. Studies in contrastive rhetoric have shown that different cultures have different ways of organizing texts and different expectations regarding the relationship between the writer and the reader (Connor & Kaplan, 1987; Hinds, 1990; Norment, 1986). Hinds (1990), for example, contends that in some cultures it is typically the writer's responsibility to make explicit all assumptions, but in other cultures it is the reader who must infer the major assumptions of the text. In learning to read and write in Vietnamese, Minh has learned certain conventions regarding text organization and reader-writer relationships. To the extent that English and Vietnamese differ in these respects, he may not meet his English audience's expectations when he applies the conventions he has learned in Vietnamese to his writing in English. In addition, he may have more difficulty reading texts that do not match his rhetorical expectations (Carrell, 1988; Carrell & Eisterhold, 1988).

Although these factors will affect Minh's acquisition of English literacy because he is literate in Vietnamese, all learners, regardless of whether or not they are literate in their native language, may have difficulty in reading English because of cultural knowledge in the text that may be unfamiliar to them. Current approaches to reading suggest that reading is an interactive process between the reader and the text that involves not only the skills to decode the symbols on the page but also the necessary background knowledge or schemata to understand the meaning of the text (Anderson & Pearson, 1988; Grabe, 1988). When Minh reads a text in English that includes a great deal of culture-specific background knowledge, his ability to understand the text may be limited by his lack of familiarity with the culture. As Gee (1990) suggests:

Types of texts and the various *ways of reading* them . . . are the social and historical inventions of various groups of people. One always and only learns to interpret texts of a certain type in certain ways through having access to, and ample experience in, social settings where texts of that type are read in those ways. (p. 45)

In order to acquire second language literacy, then, Minh will need to learn the social practices that govern the use of texts as well as the cultural information contained in such texts.

To understand how the perspective one has of literacy will frame what it means for Minh to become English literate, we turn now to a discussion of two prevalent ways of viewing literacy, namely either as an individual skill or as a social practice. For those who approach literacy as an individual accomplishment, literacy is taken to be a skill that is acquired by an individual, generally within an educational context, utilizing oral language as a basis and ultimately affecting cognitive development. As we shall see shortly, Street (1984) terms this view an *autonomous model* of literacy. Viewed from this perspective, discussions of literacy often involve a delineation of skill level and an examination of the relationship between oral and written language as well as between literacy and cognitive development. The focus is on the individual rather than on the larger social context in which the individual operates.

For those who view literacy as a social practice, what is meant by literacy depends upon the historical, economic, political, and socio-cultural context in which the learner operates. Seen from this perspective, what literacy is cannot be separated from how literacy is used by individuals within their community and how it is valued. Thus, the fact that some societies put a high economic value on literacy while others do not or that some cultures depend heavily on written language to transmit knowledge while others do not is central to defining literacy.

It is important to point out that no view of literacy is neutral. As Auerbach (1991) notes:

There can be no disinterested, objective, and value-free definition of
literacy: The way literacy is viewed and taught is always and inevitably
ideological. All theories of literacy and all literacy pedagogies are
framed in systems of values and beliefs which imply particular views of
the social order and use literacy to position people socially. (p. 71)

Both of the perspectives just discussed reflect an ideology. For Therborn (1980), an ideology addresses three central concerns: first, the question of epistemology (i.e., what exists and doesn't exist, what is true and real); second, the question of values and standards (i.e., what is good and right); and third, the question of expectations, which is intimately related to issues of power (i.e., what is possible and not possible) (as cited in Berlin, 1988, p. 479).

Both perspectives, as we shall see, reflect a set of assumptions regarding what literacy is, what its value is, and how it is related to issues of power. In the first perspective, literacy is generally regarded as a skill with important value in developing an individual's cognitive abilities, but little or no relevancy to issues of power. In the second perspective, literacy is generally regarded as a social practice that has value to both the individual and community and is closely related to issues of power. In order to understand the differences between these two perspectives, we turn to consider some of the issues that are addressed by those who view literacy as an individual skill.

An individual skill perspective

Defining the skill

Kaestle (1990) points out three debates that often underlie a definition of literacy as a skill. The first debate is between those who define literacy as a dichotomous variable and those who define it as a range of skills. Within this debate, "people who think of literacy as an either-or proposition tend to talk about problems of the illiterate and argue about how many people are illiterate. People who think of literacy as a range of skills talk about problems of literacy, not illiteracy" (p. 64). In this framework, if literacy is taken as a dichotomous variable, Minh would be categorized either as literate or illiterate, depending on whether or not he attained a certain cutoff point. (As we shall see in Chapter 2, literacy as a dichotomous variable is a perspective that is often adopted in assessing the extent of a national literacy problem in which such factors as grade level attainment serve as the cutoff point.) On the other hand, if literacy is viewed as a range of skills, Minh might be categorized as having a literacy problem if he does not meet a particular skill level defined by the various contexts in which he must use English. For example, Minh may be considered to have a so-called literacy problem in relation to a particular job if his employer feels he lacks the necessary skills to perform the job even though he has passed specific literacy courses.

A second debate underlying a definition of literacy as a skill is whether literacy consists of skills that vary on a single continuum or whether it is a collection of discrete skills. According to Kaestle (1990), in defining literacy, "those who think that literacy abilities lie along a single continuum tend to emphasize school-based literacy and grade level equivalents. Conversely, the concept of distinct literacy skills encourages one to explore nonschool uses of literacy and to incorporate in school training a detailed analysis of different reading skills needed by adults" (p. 65). In this debate, if literacy is viewed on a single continuum, Minh's English literacy skills would be assessed in reference to a school-level attainment. On the other hand, if literacy is viewed as a collection of skills, his literacy would be assessed in reference to nonschool tasks that may be job, consumer, or community oriented.

The final debate that Kaestle delineates involves a disagreement over whether literacy is purely skill based or whether it also entails some content knowledge. Those who support the latter position, such as Hirsch (1987) in the United States, contend that literacy involves a knowledge of a corpus of common literary, historical, and scientific facts. Viewed from this perspective, for Minh to be considered English literate, in addition to acquiring skill in dealing with the printed word, he would need to acquire a core of common cultural knowledge of an Anglophone culture. These various debates then illustrate that what it means to label Minh as English illiterate or English literate greatly depends on the perspective of those who are defining the terms.

Levels of literacy

Those who view literacy as a skill often posit various levels of literacy. Venezky (1990), for example, divides literacy into *"basic literacy . . . ,* which applies to the level that allows self-sustained development in literacy; and *required literacy,* which is the literacy level required for any given social context and which might, therefore, change over time, place, and social condition" (p. 11). According to this distinction, Minh will have attained basic English literacy when he can continue to develop his English literacy skills on his own. Whether or not he attains required literacy will depend on the specific demands of a particular social context such as work or school.

To meet educational programmatic needs, those who view literacy as an individual skill and focus on second language literacy often specify levels of literacy skill based on a student's mother-tongue literacy. Bell and Burnaby (1984), for example, describe how many programs categorize students in the following manner. First, there are *illiterate* students who have had a maximum of two or three years of schooling in their mother tongue. These students are divided into nonliterates who speak a language for which there is a written form and preliterates who speak a language for which there is no written form. Second, there are *semiliterate* students who have had up to eight years of formal education in their mother tongue but who often lack study skills. Third, there are *functionally nonliterate* students who have only basic literacy skills in their own language, giving them the concept of words and sentences. And finally, there are *non–roman alphabetic* students whose native language is not written in the roman alphabet and who may fall into any of the previous categories (pp. 3–6).

Although such categories were designed to meet educational programmatic needs and may be useful in this context, they are difficult to apply in reference to Minh. Given these categories, the fact that Minh is literate in Vietnamese and has a professional degree makes it difficult to know which one of the categories applies because he has had too much education to fit into either the semiliterate or functionally nonliterate category. In addition, it is extremely important that all the categories be prefaced with a language since, in Minh's case, for example, he is highly literate in Vietnamese though not so in English. As we shall see in Chapter 5, at times educational program needs for grouping students can mask the complexity of second language literacy.

Read and Mackay (1984) provide another manner of viewing second language literacy related to the level of skill one attains in the second language. These levels include *initial* literacy or "the ability to write one's own name"; *basic* literacy or the ability to "read and write a short simple sentence on . . . everyday life"; *survival* literacy or the "ability to read, write and comprehend texts on familiar subjects and to understand whatever signs, labels and instructions and directions are necessary to get along within one's environment"; *functional* literacy or "the possession of skills perceived as necessary by particular persons and groups to fulfill their own self-determined objectives"; and finally, *technical* literacy or the "acquisition of a body of theoretical or technical knowledge and the development of problem-solving capacities within that specialized field" (pp. 5–6).

Whereas Read and Mackay frame functional literacy as based on an individual's self-determined objectives, others who use this term see functional literacy as externally determined by society. Thus, what a level means depends on who is defining the term. Viewed from Read and Mackay's taxonomy, Minh's second language literacy goal is to achieve technical literacy in the medical field. However, the fact that his teacher has chosen to focus on survival literacy, seeing this as the need of the group of students in which Minh has been placed, may lead Minh to feel that his own agenda for second language literacy is not being met.

Delineating English literacy levels has also been undertaken in terms of school-based literacy for native English speakers; these categories become important when second language learners are enrolled in academic settings where school-based literacy skills are stressed. Wells (1987), for example, describes four levels of literacy: the *performative,* which involves an individual's ability to decode a written message into speech in order to ascertain its meaning; the *functional,* which entails the ability to deal with the demands of everyday life that are expressed in the written word; the *informational,* which involves the ability to process the written word in order to attain information; and finally, the *epistemic,* which entails the ability to act upon and transform knowledge and experience that are not available to those who are illiterate (pp. 110–111).

As was pointed out earlier, the informational and epistemic levels often are culturally defined. In other words, culturally defined standards may govern the presentation of information in a text or the transformation of knowledge in the process of writing. Although Minh has attained informational and epistemic literacy in Vietnamese, if, at some point, he enrolls in academic classes where these literacy levels are stressed, the question of cultural differences will become an issue and a potential source of conflicting assumptions for him.

Whereas all of the taxonomies listed thus far are set forth as hierarchical levels of literacy skills, it is important to note that the ability of an individual to attain one of the specified levels is not just a matter of acquiring a specific skill level; rather, the acquisition of various levels is often associated with different identities (Street, 1991). The attainment of what Wells terms the epistemic level can provide one with the identity of an academically educated individual; the attainment of what Read and Mackay call technical literacy can define one as a specialist in a particular field of study. In this way, the level of literacy an individual attains affects that individual's perceived role in the society. Minh in this case believes that acquiring technical literacy will provide him with the proper "identity" to be hired as a medical technologist.

However, as we shall see in subsequent chapters, acquiring this identity will require not only that Minh master the reading and writing skills necessary to operate as a medical technologist but also that he be familiar with the social practices that surround medical uses of the printed word. Gee (1991) refers to such social practices as *Discourse* with a capital *D.* For him, Discourse

is a socio-culturally distinctive and integrated way of thinking, acting, interacting, talking, and valuing connected with a particular social identity or role, with its own unique history, and often with its own distinctive "props" (buildings, objects, spaces, schedules, books, etc.). (p. 33)

Written and oral language

In addition to specifying various literacy levels, those who approach literacy as an isolated individual skill frequently examine the relationship between written and oral language as well as the relationship between literacy and cognitive development. Following in the tradition of Goody (1977) and Ong (1982), some researchers maintain that there are inherent differences between oral and written language. As Wells (1987) puts it:

In moving from speech to writing, more is involved than simply a change in the channel (oral/aural, manual/visual) through which the linguistic message is expressed. As a result of the change of mode, the nature of the message itself changes, in response both to the different purposes the two modes usually serve and to the inter- and intrapersonal contexts in which they are typically used. Writing is not simply speech written down. (p. 112)

For Wells (1987), one reason for the significant difference that exists between oral and written language arises from the fact that conversation "is jointly constructed in a shared social context in which the participants can assume a considerable amount of shared information. . . . By contrast, sustained prose is written by a writer who is distant in time and space from his or her potential readers; he or she can therefore make far fewer assumptions about shared information and has no immediate feedback from which to check that the reader's interpretation matches his or her own meaning intentions" (p. 113).

Wells's statement characterizes the typical relationship that English academic writers have with their audience – one in which it is assumed that because writers are removed, they must make explicit all of their assumptions. Yet, as was pointed out earlier, not all cultures share this view of the writer-audience relationship. To the extent that Minh holds a different set of assumptions about a writer-audience relationship, he may experience another source of conflict in acquiring second language literacy. As he gains proficiency in writing English, his English-speaking audience may assume that he also shares all of their expectations about writer-audience relationships, not realizing that proficiency in the language does not necessarily mean that one shares the same set of audience expectations.

Whereas some researchers such as Wells emphasize the differences in the audience relationship between written and oral language, other researchers maintain that one of the essential differences between written and oral language is that the permanence of the written word allows language to become an object of awareness. Olson (1990), for example, argues that literacy

is in principle a metalinguistic activity. . . . literacy turns language into
an object of awareness. . . . In the same way that language makes
objects and events in the world objects of awareness, so literacy makes
language an object of awareness. (p. 20)

By making language an object of awareness and separating the
speaker from his or her speech, Olson (1990) contends that literacy
allows the production of an "autonomous text" or authorless text
exemplified by such things as encyclopedias or school textbooks.
What is unique about such texts is that "there is no indication of the
fact that each of those statements is in fact an assertion by an author –
a speech act" (p. 21).

The idea of an "autonomous text" may be common in English, but
in some languages the concept of an autonomous text may be nonexistent. [See, for example, Osterloh (1986) for a discussion of the
close identification of an author and a text in many Arabic-speaking
cultures.] Missing then from some discussions of high-level literacy
abilities is an exploration of the ways in which literacy operates within
a cultural context. Yet such cultural differences may be a source of
conflict for Minh in his attempt to achieve second language literacy.

Literacy and cognitive development

Researchers who view literacy as an individual skill do not limit their
examination of literacy to the relationship between written and oral
language. Following the tradition of Goody and Watt (1968) and Olson
(1977), frequently they examine the relationship between literacy and
cognitive development, contending that the ability to process the written word has a profound impact on cognitive development transforming the mind and creating the ability to think independently and
abstractly, a view that, as we shall see, has been disputed by Scribner
and Cole (1981). Although some concede that cognitive development
is possible with oral language, they maintain that the written language
allows for greater cognitive benefits. Wells (1987), for example,
argues that

certainly, composing in speech may also be an aid to thought just as one
may be led to reorganize one's thinking in listening to the speech of
others. However, if the skills of transforming thoughts and knowledge
are not dependent on having learned to read and write, they are most ef-

fectively extended and developed through engaging in these more reflective modes of language use. (p. 113)

Others maintain that the acquisition of literacy, because it requires people to function independently, offers unique benefits to cognitive development. According to Cumming (1990), these unique cognitive benefits include the ability to view texts schematically, to use problem-solving strategies to control thinking while reading and writing, and finally, the ability to transform knowledge gained in reading and writing into new understandings and ideas (p. 37). In their work on literacy and bilingualism, Williams and Snipper (1990), on the other hand, dispute the idea that language influences cognition. Rather they maintain that at best there is a "reciprocal relationship between language and cognition, in that they exert some mutual, minimal influence on each other" (p. 80).

The linking of literacy to cognitive development can result in the highly questionable conclusion that those who are not literate are in some ways cognitively less able. For some, the fact that an individual is not literate suggests that this individual does not have the cognitive development that people with literacy skills have, particularly the "high" levels of literacy skills outlined earlier. Fingeret (1984), for one, disputes such a view, noting that

illiterate adults are seen not only as nonfunctional, but also as unable to take their place in society with the dignity accorded to all human beings. Although literacy educators strive to respect illiterate adults, the larger society still tends to equate illiteracy with more primitive cognitive abilities. (p. 12)

For Minh, a major frustration may be that, although he has achieved a high level of literacy in his native language and the supposed cognitive benefits that accompany this, such cognitive ability will not be valued in his Anglophone country until he has acquired sufficiently high levels of second language literacy to demonstrate this ability. Until then, his lack of English literacy may be viewed by some as an indication that he lacks the supposed unique cognitive benefits that accompany literacy.

An examination of the relationship between oral and written language, as well as the relationship between literacy and cognition, is often undertaken within a theoretical framework in which literacy is viewed essentially as an individual phenomenon. Such questions as how literacy differs cross-culturally, how it is used outside the educational structure, or to what extent literacy is valued by the society are not the major focus. These questions are examined instead by those who see literacy as embedded within a sociohistorical context. We turn now to some of the issues raised within this perspective.

A sociohistorical perspective

A historical perspective

Those who approach literacy from a historical perspective point out that both the value a society places on literacy and also the definition of literacy differ over time. Graff (1979), for example, points out that in nineteenth-century Canada, many high-level commercial posts could be held by an illiterate person if the bureaucratic record keeping could be done by someone else; the main criteria for holding the high posts were the social skills imparted in private education and a middle-class environment. In this way social skills were more valued than literacy.

The value a society places on literacy can change over time, as can the standards of literacy that are employed. For example, in the United States during World War II, one had to have a fourth-grade reading level to be admitted into the army. However, by the 1980s, the criterion for admission had changed to a high school degree (Mikulecky, 1990). Such changes occurred because as more and more individuals mastered basic literacy, it became possible to communicate information in print more easily. More complex written information became part of the society. In some ways, as Mikulecky (1990) points out, rising literacy demands are similar to what happens in a crowd when the front row rises. Everyone else has to rise in order to see and participate (p. 27).

Because of rising literacy demands, Christie (1990) contends that the literacy of the twentieth century is a far more complex phenomenon than the literacy of earlier periods. As she puts it:

Literacy in today's world is a very different thing from what it was either at the turn of the century or even mid-century. The contemporary world demands a level of sophistication in literacy greater than at any time in the past. It demands a people capable not only of handling the awesome range of print materials now a feature of a technologically advanced society, but also of creating and responding to new ones, for we do keep generating new kinds of writing, new kinds of genres, as a necessary part of generating new knowledge and new ways of thinking. (p. 21)

Viewed from a historical perspective, what it means to be literate is dependent on the literacy values and standards of the period. Individuals who do not attain the level of literacy skills valued by a society at a particular time are often viewed as "illiterate" in the sense that they are unable to meet the literacy demands required at that time. In this view the literacy demands Minh faces are a product of a twentieth-century technological society.

An economic perspective

When literacy is highly valued by a society, there may be economic advantages to becoming literate for the individual and for society. The relationship between literacy and economic benefits is the focus of those who approach literacy from an economic perspective. Central to an economic perspective of literacy is the contention that the nature of work today has changed, which makes it economically undesirable to have an illiterate population. As Fingeret (1990) notes in reference to the U.S. context:

The contemporary line of reasoning claims that we are moving into an Information Age in which technological competence is central and mobility essential. Workplaces will have to change quickly to accommodate new technologies in order to remain competitive, and literacy is necessary for both learning and doing these new jobs. . . . In this scenario, illiterate adults, unable to work in these workplaces of the future, will keep America from ascending to the top of the new global order. (p. 36)

This economic valuing of literacy is often reflected in government policies. The Australian National Policy on Languages that will be examined in Chapter 2, for example, specifically stressed the economic benefits of implementing a literacy policy by focusing "on the labour market and the ways in which tackling adult illiteracy levels, extending English proficiency and teaching 'trade languages' would benefit Australia's economic performance" (lo Bianco, 1990, pp. 48–49). When literacy is valued by a society for its economic rewards, a government is often willing to invest capital in promoting literacy by supporting classes such as the one in which Minh was enrolled, believing that such programs will encourage individuals to become economically self-sufficient. In Chapter 3 we will examine specific job-training programs supported by Anglophone countries.

Individuals who are striving to attain second language literacy, as well as those who are involved in teaching literacy, can also view literacy as an economic asset. Levine (1990), for example, maintains that "for many learners and sponsors alike, foreign language fluency appears primarily as human capital, that is, a relatively short-term investment of money and effort to enhance skills that will bring about various occupational returns (higher forms of productivity to the employer, higher remuneration to the employee) over the career as a whole" (p. 13).

What is unfortunate is that Minh, like many immigrants, may believe that his effort to achieve second language literacy will necessarily result in a well-paying job; in fact, as we shall see in Chapter 3, a variety of other factors may be far more important to obtaining this job. Graff (1979), for one, questions the "myth" that literacy leads to social mobility. Based on his study of nineteenth-century Canadian workers, he contends that the extent to which literacy during that period was beneficial was related more closely to race and ethnic background than to literacy per se.

It may be, then, that even if Minh achieves a high level of literacy, other factors such as ethnicity and race may ultimately determine his success in obtaining a job. A major assumption he may make regarding the economic benefits of literacy may therefore be undermined by other factors in the society. In fact, in the United States today, race and gender, rather than literacy per se, appear to be the prime factors in economic possibilities. This is evidenced by the 1980 U.S. Census figures which show that the median weekly salary for white males with only a high school education was higher than that of black male college graduates which, in turn, was higher than that of women of all races with some graduate school training (Auerbach, 1991, p. 74). The fact that literacy alone is not sufficient for economic rewards leads some to consider the political nature of literacy.

A political perspective

Those who view literacy as political in nature maintain that literacy both positions individuals in society and provides a means to change society. Literacy positions people in the sense that common social labels such as illiteracy can marginalize individuals. On the other hand, those who support a political perspective of literacy, such as Freire (1970), maintain that literacy can empower people to change their lives. For Freire, "learners are sociohistorical, creative, and transformative beings, and literacy is the process through which these learners can come to critically reflect on reality and take actions to change oppressive conditions. The ultimate goal of literacy is thus empowerment and social transformation" (Walsh, 1991, p. 15).

Recently in the United States, the Freirian view of literacy has resulted in what is termed a critical approach to literacy. Those who support this approach contend that education should always involve intervention. In essence the approach depends upon students' questioning and challenging the existing social order. Such critical examination "entails developing strategies to analyze the multiple ways race, ethnicity, class, gender and language are used in school to serve dominant interests" (Walsh, 1991, p. 18). By using literacy to critically examine the existing social order, this approach, according to Walsh,

makes possible an expansion of what it means to be literate beyond a functional capacity to read and to write. In other words, it fosters a reading of reality itself which goes beyond merely producing or reproducing the existing social relations and the "legitimate" knowledge which schools frame but instead encourages learners to look at the world around them in critical ways . . . and to know that their actions and involvement can make a difference. (p. 18)

Viewed from a political perspective, the labeling of Minh as English illiterate would be evidence of one way the social order has positioned and marginalized him. The goal of literacy education would be for Minh to critically reflect on his situation and to use his literacy as a basis for action.

Those who approach literacy from a historical, economic or political perspective focus primarily on how the larger society values literacy. Such perspectives often inform and challenge social policies regarding literacy. Another aspect of the relationship between society and literacy, however, is examined by those who study how literacy is used within various communities of the society. We turn now to a discussion of some of the literacy issues that are addressed in this framework.

A sociocultural perspective

Those who approach literacy from a sociocultural perspective focus "on literacy as a social and cultural phenomenon, something that exists between people and something that connects individuals to a range of experiences and to different points in time" (Schieffelin & Cochran-Smith, 1984, p. 4). One of the main proponents of such a view is Street (1991), who sets forth what he calls an *ideological model* of literacy, which recognizes a multiplicity of literacies in which "the meaning

and uses of literacy practices are related to specific cultural contexts"
(p. 1). He contrasts this with what he calls the *autonomous model* of
literacy which "assumes a single direction in which literacy development can be traced, and associates it with 'progress,' 'civilisation,'
individual liberty and social mobility. . . . It isolates literacy as an
independent variable and then claims to be able to study its consequences.
These consequences are classically represented in terms of economic
'take-off' or in terms of cognitive skills" (Street, 1984, p. 2).

Street criticizes two tenets of the autonomous model, assumptions that
were discussed earlier: first, that oral and written language are very
different, and second, that literacy per se is related to cognitive development. Street (1984) contends that within specific cultural contexts, oral
and written language assume certain functions in which "there is an
overlap and a 'mix' of modes of communication" (p. 110). He points out,
for example, that in nineteenth-century Canada, visual signs and decora-
tions were as important as letters and written words for finding one's way
around. In light of such examples, Street argues that what he calls the
"great divide" between oral and written language has been exaggerated
and that in fact the uses made of the written language in some societies
can be easily handled by oral language in others.

Street (1984) also disputes the claim that literacy per se is beneficial
to cognitive development. Street argues that because the introduction
of literacy is generally accompanied by new forms of social organization, differences in cognitive processes may not be owing to literacy
per se but rather to the new forms of social interaction that arise to
foster literacy (p. 103). He cites the work of Scribner and Cole (1981)
who studied the Vai people of Liberia, where certain literacies were
taught through individual teaching and not in schools. Scribner and
Cole found that nonliterates performed as well as or better than literates on many tasks. The only tasks that those Vai who were literate
without schooling did better on were tasks closely related to skills they
had used in becoming literate. They could, for example, use language
as a means of instruction in discussions of grammar or board games.
Furthermore, in comparing Vai, Arabic, and English literacy, all of
which existed among the Vai, they found that some cognitive skills
were enhanced by practice in specific scripts. For example, those who
were literate in Arabic and had learned the language through
memorization of the *Qur'an* were better at tasks demanding rote memorization. Thus, for Street, the way language is used and the kinds of
cognitive skills that are developed are related to social practices surrounding the use of literacy.

A major tenet of those who support a sociocultural perspective of literacy is that literacy practices, such as evaluating a book or movie, involve particular kinds of thinking that can take place in either written or oral language; thus literacy is not merely reading and writing. Langer (1987), for example, contends that the rapid developments in the mass media and computers have blurred the narrow definition of literacy as an act of reading and writing so that

a focus on simple reading and writing skills as defining "literate" thinkers, and on uses of oral and written language as involving different intellectual dimensions, are unhelpful distinctions. Uses of oral and written language mix and blur and vary as the language situation changes, and these complexities need to be considered if we are to understand the literacy demands that occur within a technological culture. (p. 4)

In addition to contending that reading and writing skills are not sufficient to attaining literate thinking but must include knowledge of the social practices in which they are embedded, those who support a sociocultural perspective further argue that "the purposes, uses and formats of literacy are varied and expanding" (Mikulecky, 1990, p. 24). Furthermore, mastering literacy in one context does not necessarily transfer to another context. Thus, the literacy promoted in schools can differ greatly from the literacy demanded in certain work contexts with little transfer between them. Indeed, Mikulecky (1990) maintains that more than a decade of research on the purposes and uses of literacy has demonstrated two factors:

Literacy processes vary widely to reflect the pluralism of social contexts in which literacy is used. Transfer of literacy abilities is severely limited by differences in format, social support networks, and required background information as one moves from context to context. (p. 25)

Viewed from a sociocultural perspective, Minh may have within his Vietnamese community a very different use of oral and written language from that which is used within his new society. Such differences may produce a source of conflict for him, particularly if his English-speaking audience assumes he shares their particular "mix" of oral and written language. Furthermore, the literacy he masters in one context (e.g., his school setting) may be of little benefit to him in other literacy contexts.

Minh, then, will experience several sources of conflict as he attempts to become literate in a second language. He and his teacher do not share the same literacy objectives. Different uses of literacy in

Vietnamese and English and different expectations regarding text organization and audience may result in his not meeting his audience's expectations. His success in achieving economic rewards for second language literacy may be undermined by other factors such as his race and ethnic background. All of these factors and others will be operating as Minh attempts to acquire second language literacy.

Summary and implications

In this chapter we have examined the difficulties that exist in defining both literacy and illiteracy, particularly as these terms apply to second language learners. We have noted that a good deal of further research is needed to determine in what way first language literacy affects the acquisition of second language literacy, although present research suggests that there is a positive transfer after one reaches a certain level of second language proficiency. We have also emphasized that being literate in a first language may result in individuals making assumptions about text development and writer-audience relationships that differ from those of English.

In exploring the plurality of literacies, we have discussed two prevalent perspectives of literacy: an individual skill perspective and a sociohistorical perspective. Those who view literacy as a skill disagree over what is included in this skill. Is it unidimensional and academically based, or does it include work-related or consumer-oriented tasks? Does it include only skills related to the printed word, or is the content used also important? Those who view literacy as a skill also distinguish various levels of skill. Some of these skill levels are identified to meet the demands of educational program placement needs. Some who view literacy as a skill also emphasize the vast differences that exist between oral and written language and contend that the printed word has important implications for cognitive development.

A second prevalent view of literacy considers literacy within a specific historical, economic, political, and cultural framework. Those who approach literacy from this perspective emphasize how definitions of literacy change over time. They give attention to the economic value of literacy both for a nation and for an individual, often reinforcing the myth that literacy alone is sufficient to lead to economic advancement. They also point out how literacy both positions people in society and can provide a means for transforming the social order.

Finally, they emphasize how various social groups have different uses of literacy and different mixes of oral and written language.

What literacy is, then, depends greatly on who is defining the term and what their purpose is. Rather than adopting a skill or a socio-historical view, it is important to recognize that both perspectives offer insights into what literacy is. It is not a question of whether literacy is a skill or a social practice; rather, literacy involves both. The challenge is to understand how the skills involved in dealing with printed matter operate in a specific individual within a social context.

What do these varying perspectives and definitions of literacy suggest for those involved in second language policymaking and education? Two important issues arise: one from the perspective of literacy as an individual skill, the other from the perspective of literacy as a social practice. First of all, frequently when literacy is used as a label in Anglophone countries, the label is applied to an individual only in reference to *English* literacy with little attention given to the existence of literacy in other languages. As Macias (1990b), for example, points out in his discussion of the United States, "policymakers, and often researchers, express a concern for literacy in general when they really mean *English* literacy (and assimilation) alone" (p. 20). Although Macias fully supports the development of English language literacy, he stresses the need to

(1) take into account the characteristics of the learner, including prior non–English language literacy ability, and (2) recognize the existence of literacy in other languages within the country, understanding that these are valuable in and of themselves as literacy, and acknowledging their utility or value as a bridge or transfer to English literacy. (p. 21)

This appeal to fully value other literacies is one that second language policymakers and educators need to seriously consider.

One specific manner in which the value of literacy in other languages can be undermined is through the use of labels for individual skill levels in educational contexts for placement and grouping purposes. Although such labels may meet pedagogical needs, they are best used if prefaced with a particular language so that it is clear when such labels are referring to English and when to another language. Illiterate is a highly charged term; therefore, it is important to use it with preciseness and care.

In reference to the perspective of literacy as a social practice, second language educators in particular need to carefully consider an important pedagogical issue that arises from this perspective. To the degree that literacy is embedded in social practices, making discourse as Gee (1991) notes, a "socio-culturally distinctive and integrated way of thinking, acting, interacting, talking, and valuing connected with a particular social identity" (p. 33), educators need to consider to what degree they believe it is necessary or desirable to develop proficiency not only in the English language but also in the ways of thinking, writing, and interacting that accompany it.

Certainly there are those who would argue that to teach such discourse is a means of assimilation. Land and Whitley (1989), for example, in reference to an academic context, argue that in striving to teach students the conventions that accompany standard written English, second language educators are requiring their students to share and reproduce in their writing a particular world view, "one to which they are, of course, alien. Such instruction is composition as colonization" (p. 289). Yet there are others who would argue that unless second language learners master such conventions, they will not have access to the social and economic opportunities that familiarity with these conventions may bring. To what extent, then, second language literacy training should involve the teaching and/or the examination of the social practices that surround it is a difficult question, one that merits much discussion and reflection.

Although, as this chapter has demonstrated, there is little agreement over what literacy is, many national leaders of Anglophone countries nevertheless believe it extremely important that the citizens of their country, both native and nonnative speakers, be literate in English. In light of this belief, they promote English literacy through a variety of national policies. The next chapter discusses three ways in which national leaders can set literacy agendas, namely through immigration and naturalization policies, literacy campaigns, and the designation of a medium of instruction in the schools. As we shall see, in general these programs and policies support Macias's contention that policy-makers' concern for literacy is a concern for English literacy with little value placed on literacy in other languages.

2 Sociopolitical agendas for second language literacy

When Carlos Cierra entered his new country, he did so without legal documents. Because of poor economic conditions at home, he was unable to find work that would provide enough income to support his family. Desperate for a job, he felt he had no other alternative but to leave home to seek employment. He entered the country without legal documents, but because of a change in legalization requirements, Carlos was eventually able to gain resident status and to bring his wife Maria and his four-year-old son Alberto into the country. Although Carlos learned English as a requirement for permanent residence, neither his wife nor son knew any English. However, they enjoyed a large community of speakers of their native language. When Alberto began school, he was placed in a class that was conducted in English.

For the Cierra family, two factors in the larger sociopolitical context – the naturalization regulations and the public school system – made it necessary for some members of the family to learn English even though all of them may have preferred to manage their lives in their mother tongue. This chapter will examine the manner in which the sociopolitical context can set literacy agendas for immigrants because of forces such as entry and naturalization requirements and school policies. After discussing the role of literacy in the sociopolitical arena, we will examine common language planning concerns of Anglophone countries. Next we will explore how these concerns are reflected in the following political decisions: overall national language policies, immigration and naturalization policies, literacy campaigns, and the designation of a medium of instruction for public schools. Throughout the chapter we will explore the conflicting agendas that underlie language planning decisions and discuss how these conflicting agendas can affect immigrants such as the Cierras.

The role of literacy in the sociopolitical arena

As was discussed in Chapter 1, an individual is considered to be literate or illiterate depending upon the social standards that are employed at the time. Today, many Anglophone countries are grappling with the question of what constitutes being English literate as opposed to illiterate. Presently in Canada, attainment of a grade nine level of education is considered to be the minimum level for functional literacy, and individuals who do not attain this level are considered to be functionally illiterate. Literacy decisions such as these are typically made by political leaders who want to have some means of measuring the extent of what is considered to be a social problem. Why do they select one criterion over another? Often such things as expediency are the determining factor. In Canada, for example, the main reason for the selection of a grade nine level of education was its ease of application (Read & Mackay, 1984, p. 14). Literacy, then, is political in nature in that the political leaders in Anglophone countries frequently define who is to be considered a literate citizen and who is not, almost always in reference to English literacy exclusively. Typically literacy is viewed as the ability of an individual to attain a certain level of education or to correctly complete items on a written examination rather than as a social practice related to a historical period or speech community.

Because the important decision of defining literate citizens is made by social and political leaders, linguists such as Gee (1990), in keeping with the social theory set forth by Foucault (1972), Habermas (1987), and others, argue that literacy is "inherently *political* (in the sense of involving relations of order and power among people)." Gee (1990) maintains that viewing literacy as the ability to read and write wrongly places literacy in the individual, "rather than in the society of which that person is a member. As such it obscures the multiple ways in which reading, writing and language interrelate with the workings of power and desire in social life" (p. 27). For Gee, when literacy is viewed as an individual skill, a good deal of the rhetoric surrounding literacy minimizes the role that a society plays in defining literacy and specifying requirements. Thus, for example, when a country proclaims a "literacy crisis," often the problem is situated in individual people who lack certain skills rather than "in the social institutions that sustain the social hierarchy and advantage elites in the society" (Gee, 1990, p. 30). Viewed from a sociopolitical perspective, although the Cierra family may not view themselves as part of a "literacy crisis," the social and political structure in defining literacy and specifying English literacy requirements may well view the Cierras as part of a national "problem." A primary way in which a society defines literacy and specifies English literacy requirements is through its language planning efforts.

Language planning

A good deal of language planning after the Second World War was undertaken by emerging nations that arose out of the end of colonial empires. These nations faced decisions as to what language(s) to designate as official for use in the political and social arena. Such language planning was often closely aligned with the desire of new nations to symbolize their newfound identity by giving official status to the indigenous language(s) (Kaplan, 1990, p. 4). Today, however, language planning has a somewhat different function. A global economy, growing poverty in some nations of the world, and wars with their resulting refugee population have resulted in great linguistic diversity in many countries. Thus, language planning issues today often revolve around attempts to balance the language diversity that exists within a nation's borders caused by immigration rather than by colonization.

In some countries, the political structure has an overall language policy that specifies the role of various languages in the society and explicitly states the country's official view toward linguistic diversity and the desired literacy level of its citizens, for instance. As lo Bianco (1990, p. 51) notes, the advantage of a stated language policy is that a set of principles has been clearly enunciated so that decisions can be made on that basis. In other countries, however, political leaders choose not to formally specify a language policy. In such instances, the educational structure may act as a *de facto* planner as state educational agencies are left to determine questions such as which language to use as a medium of instruction and what programs to establish for those who are not literate in the language of instruction. Regardless of whether or not language policies are formally stated, schools are central institutions in implementing such policies. As Huebner (1987) points out, "since responsibility for the teaching of literacy is most often assumed by schools of one kind or another, . . . language policy and planning decisions overlap to a considerable degree with educational policy and planning decisions" (p. 178). In this way, general language planning decisions and language-in-education decisions constantly interact with one another.

What are some of the major language and language-in-education planning decisions that set literacy agendas for immigrants such as the Cierras? One major decision involves the specification of the status of the various languages spoken in the country. If one language is designated as the official language, language planners need to determine the role of various other languages spoken in the country. Often when a language is designated as an official language, there is an implicit assumption that immigrants to the country should learn this language. This assumption is enacted through immigration and naturalization requirements. Two additional language planning decisions that directly involve educational issues are (1) whether or not the government should deal directly with issues of adult literacy through literacy campaigns and government-supported programs and (2) what language or languages should be used as the medium of instruction in the schools. Each of these decisions will be examined shortly. Before doing so, however, it is important to point out that underlying each of these decisions is the important question of who makes these decisions and for what purpose.

As Luke, McHoul, and Mey (1990) point out, in trying to determine what issues of social power underlie a language decision:

we can ask the rudimentary question of "whose language" is being planned, and correlatively, "whose language" is the controlling norm or guideline for such planning. This question boils down to asking *who* is planning *for whom,* and *what* (overt and covert) *aims* planning pursues; similarly, *whose behavior* is to be the standard of language use, and *what aims* such a use should set for itself. (p. 29)

Phillipson (1992) uses the term *English linguistic imperialism* to describe a situation in which "the dominance of English is asserted and maintained by the establishment and continuous reconstitution of structural and cultural inequalities between English and other languages" (p. 47).

As we shall see in this chapter, in the case of the Cierra family, the role of language in their lives will be planned in many ways by the elite of the dominant English-speaking community. To a great extent, these individuals will decide such questions as what language or languages the Cierras will need to learn for citizenship and what language or languages their children will need to learn in school. In order to illustrate how overall language policies, whether stated or unstated, can affect immigrants such as the Cierras, we turn now to an examination of the national language policies of two Anglophone nations. The first country, Australia, has chosen to specify its language policy whereas the second, the United States, has left such policies largely unstated.

National language policies

Stated policies: Australia

Although prior to the Second World War, Australian immigration favored immigrants from Britain and other European countries, during the 1960s Australia began to have a much more diverse immigrant population coming from southern Europe, the Middle East, and Asia (Tollefson, 1991, p. 173). Concerned about the low educational and economic status of recent immigrants, in 1977 Prime Minister Malcom Fraser appointed a committee chaired by Frank Galbally to review the services available to this population. Although the report emphasized that Australia should end its long emphasis on assimilation and adopt a policy of multiculturalism, which allowed individuals to maintain their culture, the committee viewed the acquisition of English as a key factor in solving immigrants' problems. As the Galbally Report stated in its recommendations:

Many of the problems encountered by migrants arise from inadequate arrangements for their initial settlement here. *We recommend a comprehensive initial settlement program* . . . which would *include classes in English and formal orientation courses including advice and assistance in housing, education, employment and other areas of need.* . . .
Because we recognize that migrants' knowledge of the English language is a critical factor in enabling successful settlement in Australia we give special attention to the teaching of English both to children and adults. (Galbally Report as cited in Foster & Stockley, 1988, p. 57)

The report recommended funds to promote community languages; however, more emphasis and funds were given to the learning of English. Because the report was not formally adopted by the government, various social groups began to lobby for a formally stated language policy. This pressure, combined with Australia's increasing trade with Asian non–English speaking countries (which made it advantageous to promote Asian languages in Australia), resulted in an Australian National Policy on Languages. This policy was endorsed by the Commonwealth under Prime Minister Hawke in 1987 (lo Bianco, 1990, pp. 55–56).

The following principles form the basis for the National Policy on Languages and its related programs. First, the policy contains a series of statements about the status of language in Australia. These begin with a recognition of Australian English as the "National, convenient and shared Language of Australia and its major official institutions." This is followed by a recognition of the rights of individuals to use a community language other than English. The main section of the policy, however, deals with educational policies that reflect three major principles: "English for All," which contains specifications for English education for native English speakers as well as for second language speakers (such as the Cierras), "Support for Aboriginal and Torres Strait Islander Languages," which entails elements of bilingual education for indigenous groups, and "A Language Other than English for All," which entails the teaching of community languages to encourage the mother tongue maintenance of immigrants as well as foreign language teaching for native English speakers. Also included in the document was an allocation of government funds for the implementation of the policy, which was intended to supplement existing state efforts in the area of language (lo Bianco, 1990, pp. 62–63).

In Australia, states and territories have jurisdiction over education, so their support was critical for the implementation of the policy. Although most states welcomed the policy, according to lo Bianco (1990), "opposition to some of its goals, especially the support for ethnic minority languages and aboriginal languages, from some sections of the broader community should not be underestimated" (p. 64). The development and implementation of the policy then took place within a context of conflicting literacy agendas. Whereas immigrant and indigenous groups actively lobbied for the establishment of their language rights, others were opposed to the granting of such rights. If one applies the standard set forth by Luke et al. (1990) for ascertaining issues of social power in language-planning decisions, it is evident that the social power rested largely in the hands of the dominant Anglophone group. Although recognition of the language rights of immigrant and indigenous groups is significant, as was nevertheless pointed out, opposition to the promotion of immigrant and indigenous languages was widespread, with the major principle of the policy being "English for All."

More recently the recognition in the National Policy on Languages of the value of promoting multilingualism has been undermined by the release of a policy paper by the Commonwealth Department of Employment, Training and Education entitled *The Language of Australia: Discussion Paper on an Australian Literacy and Language Policy for the 1990s.* This paper, as suggested by its title with the singular use of *language,* approaches literacy solely in terms of English literacy, giving no recognition to the value of immigrants developing literacy in their mother tongue. Those who support the policies outlined in the paper maintain that promoting English literacy among all citizens will help people get jobs and reverse the balance of trade figures. Thus, the major rationale for the language policy outlined in the paper is an economic one. This influence of economic agendas on the formation of language policies is one that we will consider more fully in the next chapter.

What impact would the Australian National Policy on Languages have on the Cierra family? First of all, in light of the major principle of "English for All," there would be an English language agenda set for the family and an English literacy requirement set for them through the educational system. In addition, there would be support for the maintenance of their mother tongue. The policy itself, however, does not carry the force of law. Because in the Australian legal system class action is highly restricted and there is no Bill of Rights, the possibility of minority language rights questions being taken into the legal arena (as in the United States) is minimal (lo Bianco, 1990, p. 63). Another effect of the policy is that there would be government funds available for the Cierras to attend English classes if they so desired. One potential benefit, then, of formalizing a language policy is that government resources may be forthcoming to support language programs consistent with the national policy. On the other hand, when a country does not specify an overall national language policy, there is less basis for pressuring government for the funding of language programs. This is the type of situation that currently exists in the United States.

Unstated policies: The United States

Whereas Australia has explicitly formulated a language policy regarding the languages spoken in that country, the United States has historically been ambivalent in its attitudes toward linguistic diversity, as Leibowitz (1984) points out.

On the one hand, the U.S. Constitution makes no mention of language. This is somewhat unusual since the designation of an official language is quite common in constitutional documents, not only in multilingual countries, but also in countries where only one language is generally used. On the other hand, John Jay in the *Federalist Papers* saw the English language as the tie that bound the federal structure. (p. 25)

Early leaders did not name an official language for a variety of reasons. First, they did not wish to restrict the linguistic and cultural freedom of those living in the country. In addition, they recognized the economic and social value of foreign language expertise. Finally, they believed that freedom of choice in language had the pragmatic advantage of serving to attract new immigrants (Judd, 1987, p. 115). Although the United States has no official language policy, the country in fact operates in most ways as if English were the official language insofar as all government proceedings are in English and the primary medium of instruction in the public schools is English.

However, periodically, particularly in times of nativism such as during the world wars, the United States has witnessed strong movements to make English the official language. The current English Only movement in the United States is one instance of this phenomenon. According to Judd (1987), those who support this amendment argue that the national unity of the country necessitates the specification of a national language. They also argue that current policies allowing for the use of language other than English encourages immigrants not to learn English and thus keeps them on the fringes of society (pp. 117–119).

If the United States does pass an English Only amendment with no protection for minority languages, what effect would such an amendment have on families such as the Cierras? First of all, the amendment could deny workers such as Carlos the use of their mother tongue on the job. Second, the law could deny the use of any language other than English in matters relating to public safety and health. And finally, the amendment could restrict bilingual education and bilingual ballots (Judd, 1987, p. 126). Passage of the amendment, however, would face several obstacles. Unlike Australia, in the United States the national Bill of Rights, which guarantees freedom of speech and the possibility of class action, would present legal challenges to the enactment of the amendment. (In fact, a federal district judge in Arizona has already ruled that the Arizona state English Only amendment is a violation of federally protected free speech rights.)

The irony is that, although the current lack of a stated national language policy in the United States is beneficial to the Cierra family in that it does not prohibit their ability to use their mother tongue in the ways they might wish to, it does little to provide resources for them to make the language choices they may like to make. On the other hand, having a stated policy, particularly if it is in conflict with their personal language agendas, will greatly restrict their choices. In either case language decisions of the social elite will affect the Cierras' own personal language and literacy agendas. In this way issues of power are intimately related to literacy choices.

Overall national language policies that specify the language objectives of a country are not the only way in which the sociopolitical arena can affect the language choices of immigrant families such as the Cierras. Another significant way in which their personal language choices can either be supported or undermined is in the enactment of national immigration and naturalization requirements. We turn now to a discussion of how these policies set language and literacy agendas and thus affect the personal agendas of families such as the Cierras.

Immigration and naturalization policies

A widely held assumption is that immigrants have an obligation to acquire the official language of their host country. As Kloss (1971, p. 254) points out, often the dominant ethnic group in a country believes it to be self-evident that immigrants ought to give up their language as quickly as possible and learn the dominant language. According to Kloss, four common arguments are given to support this view. First, those who advocate learning the dominant language argue that in return for a country's accepting immigrants, it is the immigrants' responsibility to accept the language and culture of the host country; thus, the immigrants must waive any minority language rights (the tacit compact theory). Second, they maintain that because most immigrants will be more prosperous than when they left their home, the immigrants owe it to the country to adopt its ways (the give-and-take theory). Third, they contend that teaching the mother tongue to the next generation may lead to the formation of linguistic ghettoes (the antighettoization theory). And finally, they argue that the unity of the nation depends on all of its members knowing the dominant language (the national unity theory).

Kloss offers counterarguments to each of these assertions. In so doing, he stresses the rights of language minorities to set their own language and literacy agendas. First of all, Kloss points out that historically countries such as Argentina, Chile, and the United States have given their immigrants ample leeway to establish their own schools. These countries in their early history did not envision any "tacit compact" that immigrants must of necessity learn the language of the

dominant culture. There is, then, historical precedence for challenging
the tacit compact theory. Second, Kloss concedes that it is perhaps true
that families such as the Cierras will be economically better off than
they were in their native country. However, he argues that immigrants
by their very presence in the country provide economic benefits to the
host country by providing labor and expanding the consumer market,
activities they can be undertaken regardless of whether the immigrants
speak or read the dominant language. Third, Kloss argues that the fact
that immigrants such as the Cierras live among members of their own
language community may in large part be owing to factors of the larger
sociopolitical structure that allow them few other options, even if they
know the language of the dominant group. Finally, Kloss points out
that the national unity of a country has generally been threatened by
language minorities only in cases where their language rights have
been denied. In sum, Kloss believes it is important to carefully consider the commonly acted upon assumption that language minorities
have a responsibility to acquire the language of the dominant culture.

Although the assumption that immigrants should learn the dominant
language is open to question, most Anglophone countries in their
entrance and/or naturalization requirements take this to be a given.
Some countries give entry preference to immigrants who speak English. The 1967 Canadian Immigration Act, for example, gives preferential points to immigrants who speak English if they enter the
country under an independent classification. More common, however,
Anglophone countries have English language and literacy agendas for
naturalization rather than immigration. The British Naturalization Act
of 1981, for example, specifies that for naturalization an individual
must have "sufficient knowledge of the English, Welsh or Scottish
Gaelic language." In some countries, such as the United States, English proficiency for naturalization is verified through a literacy examination. In order to illustrate the manner in which immigration and
naturalization regulations allow the sociopolitical structure to set
literacy agendas, we will examine the literacy requirements for U.S.
immigration and naturalization.

Immigration and naturalization policies in the United States

In his analysis of the literacy requirements for immigration and naturalization in the United States, Leibowitz (1984) points out that although
the United States had unrestricted immigration until the fourth quarter
of the nineteenth century, from the time of the founding of the Republic,

federal policy placed conditions on naturalization, for example, by imposing a long qualifying period for citizenship. It was not, however, until the twentieth century that there was serious discussion about an English literacy requirement for naturalization. In 1905, owing to charges of bribery and fraud in gaining naturalization, President Roosevelt commissioned a major study of naturalization procedures and requirements. This committee recommended an English literacy requirement for naturalization.

Two years later, a Federal Immigration Commission recommended that a literacy test be required for immigration. However, the commission proposed that the test could be taken in any language, not just English. At the basis of the recommendation for a literacy test was the belief that current immigrants were very different from old immigrants who had quickly become assimilated. In contrast, the new immigrants were less intelligent and willing to learn English. As the commission put it:

... the new immigration has been largely a movement of unskilled laboring men who have come in large part temporarily, from the less progressive and advanced countries of Europe in response to the call for industrial workers in the eastern and middle western states. . . .

The new immigration as a class is far less intelligent than the old, approximately *one third of all those over 14 years of age when admitted being illiterate.* Racially, they are for the most part essentially unlike the British, German and other peoples who came during the period prior to 1880, and generally speaking they are actuated in coming by different ideals, for the old immigrants came to be part of the country, while the new, in large measure, comes with the intention of profiting, in a pecuniary way, by the superior advantages of the new world and then returning to the old country. (as cited in Leibowitz, 1984, p. 36)

The commission's recommendation resulted in the passage of legislation requiring literacy tests in any language for immigration in 1913 and again in 1915. However, both of these bills were vetoed by Presidents Taft and Wilson, who emphasized the racial impact of such legislation. It was not until 1917 that a similar bill was passed by Congress over Wilson's second veto. According to Leibowitz (1984, p. 43), the immigration literacy test of 1917 marked a major transition in the development of U.S. immigration policy because its basic intention was to use literacy to reduce the number of immigrants, particularly those from southeastern Europe, who were considered racially unlike the British, German, and other peoples who had come earlier. Thus, literacy in the United States began to be used for racial purposes. In

1924 an Immigration Act was passed that did not change the literacy test requirement but added quota systems based on the U.S. population as it existed at the time, a policy that was clearly based on racial principles.

In subsequent years various court decisions overturned some of the literacy test legislation but sustained English literacy as a requirement for naturalization. To qualify for naturalization today, there is an English literacy requirement, along with the requirement of demonstrating knowledge of U.S. history and government. In reviewing immigration and naturalization law, Leibowitz (1984) contends that the laws were basically racially motivated. As he puts it:

Both the literacy requirement for immigration and the English literacy requirement for naturalization had at their root a racial purpose. They were reinforced by a series of other statutes imposing English language requirements as a condition for access to the American political and economic life. (p. 58)

United States literacy requirements, in regard to immigration and naturalization, illustrate how literacy is related to issues of race. Furthermore, the historical development of these policies demonstrates how the gatekeeping function of English literacy has expanded from serving no function in citizenship to now being necessary for naturalization.

Racial issues and an expansion of the gatekeeping function of English literacy in U.S. naturalization law are more recently evident in the 1986 Immigration Reform and Control Act, which provides the opportunity for undocumented individuals who meet certain requirements to become legal citizens. Under this legislation, in order to qualify for legal residence, undocumented individuals must demonstrate proficiency in English and an understanding of U.S. history and government through a written examination or show that they are making satisfactory progress in a course of study that is certified to fulfill such requirements (Wrigley, 1988, p. 1).

A number of advocacy groups oppose the regulation, pointing out that requiring individuals who seek permanent residence, and not citizenship, to demonstrate a knowledge of English and U.S. history and government is not typical and in essence discriminates against this population (Wrigley, 1989, p. 1). Furthermore, such groups believe that the mandatory course of study will cause a hardship for many students. Although it is now possible for students to waive the course requirement by taking a test, originally the testing procedure was not standardized, with the result that arbitrary questions (such as asking for the names of political leaders, their spouses, or even their horses) were included (Wrigley, 1988, p. 7). The test option, however, is not available to a large number of persons seeking amnesty who are not literate in English. For these individuals, the only option available is to attend classes and learn to read and write in English in order to receive a certificate of attendance. In the following chapter we will review some of the economic reasons for the passage of such legislation. For now it is important to point out how political policies such as these set English literacy agendas for individual immigrants, suggesting that the only literacy of value is English literacy. In addition, it is important to note that once again in the United States the gatekeeper function of literacy has expanded. The result is that, although originally English literacy served no purpose for entry or naturalization, today it is used not only for naturalization but also in some cases for permanent residency.

In the case of the Cierra family, regulations such as those contained in the 1986 Immigration Reform and Control Act greatly restrict their options. The only possibility for Carlos to achieve a reunification of his family in a place where he has employment is for him to apply for permanent residence. In so doing, he will be required to demonstrate, either through a course of study or a test, English literacy and an understanding of U.S. history and government. In this way, his own personal agenda for supporting and raising a family can be met only if he satisfies the political agenda of his host country to learn to read English and demonstrate knowledge of the history of the country as a way of showing his allegiance. The options he has available arose in large part owing to factors beyond his control, namely the poor economic conditions of his native country. Thus, although he may initially have had no goal of achieving second language literacy, political and economic conditions made it necessary for him to do so.

Another major way in which sociopolitical agendas can affect the life of the Cierra family, both adults and children, is in the area of public policies on education. A literacy agenda will be set for Alberto when he enters school and will determine whether his initial literacy training will be in his mother tongue or in English. Carlos and Maria, on the other hand, may be affected by a national concern for adult literacy. In order to illustrate what effect such national concern can have on their lives, we turn now to an examination of literacy campaigns in Anglophone countries.

Literacy campaigns

Periodically Anglophone countries launch national literacy campaigns. Such a campaign was undertaken in the 1970s in Great Britain. In 1983 the president of the United States established an Initiative on Adult Literacy that resulted in a National Literacy Project (Fingeret, 1984, p. 1). In 1987 the Australian government's endorsement of the National Policy on Languages gave prominence to the issue of adult literacy, resulting in a two-year campaign to improve the level of adult literacy. What are the possible effects of these and other campaigns on immigrant families such as the Cierras?

To begin, such campaigns reinforce a particular social view of literacy, one in which a lack of English literacy is often viewed as a social and economic problem. As lo Bianco (1989, pp. vii–viii) points out, traditionally adult literacy has been viewed as an individual problem, at times related to welfare issues. He contends that more recently attention has been given to the economic costs to a nation of having illiterate citizens. Such views are evident in Morey's (1989) discussion of the individual and social consequences of "inadequate literacy" for Australia. Included in his list of consequences are such things as the following:

On a broad level, deficiencies in literacy diminish the skills of the workforce as a whole, indirectly affecting national economic growth.

Illiteracy restricts personal advancement and industrial flexibility. . . .

Illiterate adults suffer decreasing employability as the number of jobs requiring only low literacy skills continues to decrease. . . .

Adults with low levels of literacy are more likely than others to be dependent on welfare. (p. 5)

The assertions contained in this list may lead to the questionable conclusion that individuals who are not literate are the cause of social and economic problems. Thus, to the extent that literacy campaigns describe literacy (phrased solely as English literacy) as a social and economic problem, individuals who cannot read and write in English may be seen as problems and marginal members of the society. In this way, one possible effect of a literacy campaign is that members of the Cierra family may be viewed as social problems even if they are gainfully employed and literate in another language.

Approaching literacy as a national problem has other repercussions. Often in such campaigns political leaders take a problem-solution approach to literacy, resulting in a need to assess the extent of the problem and arrive at a solution. In trying to assess the extent of the problem, a definition of literacy is needed in order to determine how many citizens are not literate. As was pointed out earlier, at times, for expediency, a measure such as grade level attainment is used. Other approaches are possible. In some instances criterion reference tests have been used, such as those in the United States Adult Performance Level Study. This study used paper-and-pencil tests that required the completion of tasks similar to those encountered by literate middle-class adults in their daily life, such as reading transportation schedules or writing a check. One of the major criticisms of the tests was that the test items implied "a particular concept of the good life" (Fingeret, 1984, p. 8). In this way, through the content of the questions, such tests assume a familiarity with mainstream ways of life in their definition of literacy. By so doing they make it necessary for families such as the Cierras to gain familiarity with the mainstream culture in order to qualify as English literate adults. In Chapter 5, we will examine in greater depth the assumptions of such tests regarding literacy.

In declaring a literacy campaign, political leaders of Anglophone countries often set objectives for the campaign. In general, these include attention to the widespread promotion of English literacy. In New Zealand, however, the objectives of recent literacy campaigns have included attention to Maori literacy. In 1990, for example, the minister of education announced an ongoing grant that was to be used specifically for Maori literacy development (Caunter, 1990, p. 51). The grant reflected the concern of several New Zealand organizations to redress the balance of power between Maoris and those of European descent (Caunter, 1990, p. 50). Australia, in its National Policy on Languages, also supports the development of aboriginal and Torres Strait Islander languages. There is, then, attention in some Anglophone countries to the promotion of literacy in the mother tongue of indigenous groups.

Both the Australian National Policy on Languages and the proposed New Zealand National Language Policy specify support for the development of literacy in community languages. However, whereas the policies stress the right of individuals to maintain their native language, they do not promote the development of such languages to the degree that they do with both English and indigenous languages. In this way the policies of Australia and New Zealand reflect different views toward the language rights of indigenous and immigrant groups. In the case of indigenous groups, both countries appear to be supporting what Kloss (1971, pp. 259–260) calls promotion-oriented rights, which involve government support for mother-tongue maintenance. In the case of immigrant groups, on the other hand, they appear to be supporting what Kloss (1971, pp. 259–260) calls toleration-oriented rights, which involve the rights of citizens in their private lives to promote their mother-tongue maintenance. Thus, in both countries, although families such as the Cierras would have the right to develop literacy in their native language, literacy in this language would not be actively promoted by the government.

In addition to setting objectives, literacy campaigns often include a "solution" to the problem in the form of a literacy program. These remedies can include mass media promotions of the campaign. Such a strategy was used in the British literacy campaign of the 1970s, when television literacy lessons called "On the Move" were followed by a telephone number that citizens could call, either to get help in gaining literacy skills or to volunteer as a tutor (Read & Mackay, 1984, p. 79).

Another solution, one that has been widely used in various Anglophone countries, is a volunteer tutor program. In Canada, for example, tutoring as a method for meeting the literacy needs of immigrant groups was supported in two major government reports, *Work for Tomorrow* and *Learning for Life*. Read and Mackay (1984, p. 69) contend that although the contribution of volunteer tutors should not be discounted, a society that depends on volunteers to address the issue of literacy does not view literacy as a basic right of its members. The benefit of such a program is, of course, an economic one. The enactment of a widespread literacy campaign composed largely of tutors can meet the demands of a "literacy crisis" while costing relatively little. However, the success of such programs is open to question.

In Great Britain, for example, even when television was widely used to publicize the problem of literacy and find tutors and learners, it was estimated that only about 7 percent of those needing literacy training had been reached and of those, 30 percent did not begin training or had dropped out after one week (Read & Mackay, 1984, p. 70). Furthermore, the British campaign, by promoting one-to-one tutoring and ensuring individuals that their work with a tutor was confidential, promoted a particular view of illiteracy. As Read and Mackay (1984) note:

The emphasis on secrecy and confidentiality stressed in this campaign tended to stress the element of shame: the sense that the individual was at fault. The predominance of one-to-one teaching reinforced this aspect. While the identities of illiterates were protected, participants rarely met each other and so missed the opportunity to provide one another with mutual support. (p. 80)

One-to-one tutoring can lead individuals such as Carlos and Maria to feel that they have a problem and that they are largely at fault for this problem even though a great many other factors, as we shall see, can affect their inability to read and write in English. In addition, one-to-one tutoring tends to reinforce the notion of literacy as solely an individual skill rather than as a range of social practices, providing little opportunity for individuals to use literacy with others to share mutual concerns and gain support.

Some literacy campaigns, rather than relying heavily on volunteer tutors, result in additional funding for government-sponsored adult literacy classes. The Australian National Policy on Languages, for example, called for additional funds being allocated for literacy programs for immigrants so that eligible students would be able to participate for up to twelve months in intensive English courses (lo Bianco, 1990, p. 65). In the United States during the last decade federal, state, and local governments have appropriated millions of dollars to support a massive adult literacy campaign. Many of the programs that have been developed in response to literacy campaigns promote basic reading and writing with the primary aim of developing functional literacy and job-related skills. Critics argue that the programs promote a very limited kind of literacy that is aimed at preparing individuals for particular life roles, often ones that involve the semiskilled labor market (Torruellas, Benmayer, Goris, & Juarbe, 1992, p. 183). In this way such programs, although fulfilling the national demand for a literate work force, limit the kind of literacy development available to language minorities. Thus, through both the view of literacy they promote and the type of programs they engender, literacy campaigns set literacy agendas for Carlos and Maria.

Carlos and Maria are not the only members of the family whose language and literacy educational choices will be affected by the sociopolitical structure. The sociopolitical structure, through its enactment of educational policies, will also affect Alberto when he begins public education. These policies will set the agenda of whether his initial literacy will be in English or in his mother tongue. In selecting a medium of instruction for public schools, language-in-education planners must decide which language to use (the mother tongue or English), at what stage of instruction to introduce the selected language or languages, and for what purpose (for full development of the language or as a transition to another language). Making these decisions has led to heated debates in many Anglophone countries. We turn now to a discussion of how this decision has been dealt with in two Anglophone countries, Great Britain and the United States.

Designation of the medium of instruction

Great Britain: mainstream classes

Although Britain, like the United States, has a long history of immigration, it was only in the early 1950s that speakers of many languages started to settle in Britain in significant numbers all at the same time. These immigrants were mainly refugees from Eastern Europe, East Africa, and Southeast Asia, as well as labor migrants from Southern and Eastern Europe and from former British colonies in South and East Asia and the Caribbean (Martin-Jones, 1989). During the 1960s, one of the first programs established by local school districts set up separate language centers (termed *induction centres*) for language minority students such as Alberto. According to Reid (1988), such students were

separated from their English-speaking peers ostensibly so that they could be taught English to a level which would allow them to join classes in ordinary schools, but also, of course, to satisfy majority parents that their children would not be "held back" by the presence of large numbers of immigrant children in the same classes. (p. 187)

Growing concern with the issue of English literacy both for native and nonnative speakers resulted in 1975 with the publication of what is known as the Bullock Report. This central government report was produced by a committee of inquiry whose primary purpose was to investigate native-speaking children's language development across the school years. However, in the chapter on the language needs of language minority children entitled "Children from Families of Overseas Origin," the committee argued that

in a linguistically conscious nation in the modern world, we should see it [the mother-tongue] as an asset, as something to be nurtured, and one of the agencies that should nurture it is the school. Certainly the school should adopt a positive attitude to its pupils' bilingualism and whenever possible should help to maintain and deepen their knowledge of their mother-tongues. (Department of Education and Science, 1975, p. 294)

Ironically, after the publication of the report, few programs were established to promote native language maintenance even though the rhetoric of the report suggested that this should be done.

In 1985, a second major educational policy statement regarding language minority students was issued with the publication of the Department of Education and Science's report, *Education for All,* commonly known as the Swann Report. This report was prepared by a national committee whose task was solely to examine educational policies for language minority students. The Swann Report strongly endorsed mainstreaming, the placing of language minority students in English-medium schools with support services. The Swann Report did not support bilingual education "principally on the grounds that to implement it, minority children would have to be segregated. They feared that this might highlight differences and have a detrimental effect on race relations" (Edwards, Moorhouse, & Widlake, 1988, p. 81). Although the Report argued that local education authorities should make school buildings available for native language instruction, the Swann Committee viewed the maintenance and development of language minority students' native language as a responsibility of the ethnic community itself rather than the school. This view reflects the toleration-oriented language rights referred to earlier rather than promotion-oriented rights. By so doing, the report provided little support for individuals such as the Cierras to pursue mother-tongue literacy, supporting Macias's contention that when policymakers express a concern for literacy, they often really mean *English* literacy (Macias, 1990b).

The Swann Report sparked substantial debate in Great Britain. The major criticisms came from advocates of instruction in the student's first language. (See, for example, Khan, 1985, and National Council for Mother Tongue Teaching, 1985.) First, the critics challenged the Swann Report's definition of *pluralism,* arguing that the report, by not advocating native language instruction in the schools, was promoting a type of linguistic assimilation in which the ability to speak English was equated with being British (National Council for Mother Tongue Teaching, 1985, p. 499). Advocates of instruction in the mother tongue lamented the fact that the Swann Report offered no support for the earlier recommendation of the Bullock Report for native language instruction in the schools. (See, for example, Devall, 1987.)

The critics further argued that the Swann Report failed to recognize the important link between first and second language development. Pointing to bilingual programs in the United States and Scandinavian countries and to the work of Cummins (1982, 1984), critics argued that the report ignored the important role that first language maintenance can have in both cognitive development and in the acquisition of a second language.

Finally, proponents of native language instruction criticized the Swann Report for its failure to see the intimate connection between language and culture. Critics argued that

in failing to recognise the intrinsic links between language and culture, the Report does not perceive the centrality of language in culture, in the development of ethnicity and of the individual's cultural identity. At the very outset of the Report, ethnic identity is described by stressing a physical attribute of race – skin color – rather than the social attribute of language. (National Council for Mother Tongue Teaching, 1985, p. 501)

Support for the Swann Report's negative stance toward bilingual education has come from the Kingman Report (Department of Education and Science, 1989), authored by the conservative forces currently controlling education in Great Britain, who contend that placing language minority students in mainstream classes benefits all students' awareness of language. More recently, the Cox Report has resulted in the writing of a national curriculum that outlines legally mandated requirements for the teaching of English. The enactment of the curriculum has been surrounded by controversy in which government leaders who espouse a back-to-basic approach to literacy development found the meaning-making, learner-centered approach set forth in the curriculum unacceptable (Richmond, 1992).

Today, then, in Britain most government reports advocate a policy of initial literacy in English with some mother-tongue support being available in mainstream classes, but the active promotion of mother-tongue literacy is left to the community. Such policies have been endorsed at least ostensibly on the grounds that they ensure cultural pluralism in the country by promoting ethnic diversity in the classroom. However, critics of current policies would argue that the lack of support in the policy for linguistic pluralism with regard to mother-tongue literacy reflects an assimilationist view of pluralism. The United States, on the other hand, at least during the 1960s and 1970s, has given some support for bilingual education programs that would foster initial literacy in the mother tongue.

The United States: bilingual education

The United States experienced a large increase in immigrants during the 1960s, largely owing to the change in immigration laws of 1965, which abandoned the national origins quota system and gave preference instead to family reunification and occupational skills. The United States has little that is comparable to the Bullock, Swann, Kingman, or Cox Reports, which set forth national language policies for language minority students such as Alberto. Rather, U.S. policies develop from constitutional, statutory, or judicial sources. One significant statutory basis for language programs for language minority students is Title VII of the 1968 Elementary and Secondary Education Act (also known as Title VII or the Bilingual Education Act). The original purpose of the Title VII program was to encourage the use of bilingual educational practices so that children such as Alberto would experience initial literacy in their mother tongue. Although this legislation provided funds for bilingual education, it did not legally guarantee language minority children the right to receive instruction in their mother tongue. Lau *v.* Nichols, a Supreme Court decision addressing the issue of the educational rights of language minorities, did not uphold the legal right of language minorities to receive bilingual education. Rather, the decision specified that the special needs of language minority students must be addressed, leaving open the kind of program that could be allowed to meet these needs. Thus, whereas bilingual education in the United States is not a right of language minorities, there are federal funds available for such programs.

The standard U.S. Department of Education definition of bilingual education is as follows:

Bilingual education is the use of two languages, one of which is English, as the medium of instruction for the same pupil population in a well-organized program which encompasses part or all of the curriculum and includes the study of the history and culture associated with the mother tongue. A complete program maintains the children's self-esteem and a legitimate pride in both cultures. (as cited in Paulston, 1980, p. 8)

Today in the United States, however, bilingual education includes an immense array of programs, some of which include a good deal of instruction in the mother tongue and some of which, in contrast to the definition just listed, include instruction only in English. In fact, in 1983, Secretary of Education Terrell Bell proposed amendments to Title VII that were designed to give school districts greater flexibility in their choice of instructional approaches, with the result that instruction in language minority students' native language was no longer a requirement for Title VII funds (Rotberg, 1984, p. 135).

One of the main controversies surrounding bilingual education programs has been whether such programs should exist solely to provide
a transition to English-only instruction or whether they should support
maintenance of the mother tongue. Those programs that do have a
maintenance objective can promote either what Otheguy and Otto
(1980, p. 351) term *static maintenance* (i.e., maintenance of the native
language skills that students have upon entering the school system) or
developmental maintenance (i.e., development of the students' native
language to the point of full proficiency and literacy in the mother
tongue). The bilingual education movement in the United States has
generated little support for developmental maintenance. Rather, even
from the beginning, the majority of programs funded under Title VII
have been transitional in nature, with the aim of raising the English
proficiency of children such as Alberto to a point where they can
participate in English-medium schools.

Spener (1988), in his assessment of transitional bilingual education
in the United States, argues that there are serious social consequences
to placing children such as Alberto in English-only classrooms after
one or two years in transitional bilingual education classes. According
to Spener (1988):

The social consequences include defining the terms of competition and
social ranking in the public schools and influencing the perceptions that
English mother-tongue students and teachers have of immigrant children in their classes. Immigrant children (as well as children of native-
born linguistic minority parents) mainstreamed into regular classrooms
from transitional bilingual programs may be presented before their
teachers and classmates not as equal-but-different representatives of
another language and culture, but rather as imperfect or inferior members of the domestic culture. (p. 149)

Thus, Spener would argue that if Alberto were placed in an English-
medium classroom after starting his schooling in a transitional bilingual
education program, he may be viewed as an "inferior" member for no
other reason than that his family speaks another language. Such programs
then can marginalize language minority children in much the same way
that literacy campaigns do, in that they promote a deficit view of language
minorities.

What are the likely consequences of the language policies of Great
Britain and the United States on Alberto? In the case of Great Britain,
Alberto would probably be placed in an English-medium school with
some type of language support service in the classroom. In the United

States, on the other hand, he might have the option of attending a bilingual program when he first entered school. However, because in most instances such programs are transitional in nature, Alberto would likely go to an English-medium class as soon as he had sufficient English proficiency to do so, a transition that, as Spener notes, may be quite difficult. In either instance, however, a personal or family literacy agenda of fully developing Alberto's mother-tongue literacy in addition to developing English literacy would be difficult to achieve. Although Great Britain and the United States differ in the extent to which they have supported bilingual education programs, the basic agenda in both countries is to develop English literacy with only marginal attention to the development of mother-tongue literacy.

In this way, the literacy choices of immigrant families are greatly restricted by the decisions made by those in power. As Tollefson (1991) puts it, for a language minority such as Alberto, the choice of whether to develop English literacy, his mother-tongue literacy, or both "does not involve 'choice' at all, if choice means the freedom to select from alternatives without coercion. Instead, his language behavior involves the dynamic interaction between his linguistic repertoire and the system of social and economic inequality in which he lives" (p. 78).

Summary and implications

In this chapter we have examined the ways in which the language and literacy choices of language minorities are circumscribed by sociopolitical literacy agendas. When a country formally adopts a national language policy, as was done in Australia, such a policy can set specific language and literacy agendas for the citizens of the country. On the other hand, when a country has no stated policy, as in the United States, the language and literacy agenda is an open question. In such cases, tradition often dictates an agenda. The sociopolitical structure can also set language and literacy agendas through its immigration and naturalization requirements. Frequently, such regulations are based on the assumption that those seeking citizenship status have an obligation to show proficiency in English literacy and in some instances an understanding of the history and culture of the country. Literacy campaigns undertaken by Anglophone countries also set literacy agendas by suggesting that those who are not literate in English are a problem that must be addressed. Finally, the sociopolitical structure, through the educational system, sets literacy agendas for young language minorities in the designation of a medium of instruction.

Political and educational leaders make the language and literacy decisions they do for a variety of reasons. In the case of overall language policies, politicians may want to ensure the dominant group that their language will remain dominant; at the same time, as in Australia, political leaders may make the decisions they do in response to the demands of minority groups. In the area of immigration and naturalization, political leaders may face pressures from the dominant group to restrict the ethnic background of immigrants who are allowed entry and citizenship. As we have seen, racial factors such as these have been evident in the U.S. immigration and naturalization policies. Literacy campaigns may be enacted by political leaders to respond to the demands of business and labor leaders for a literate work force. The designation of a medium of instruction may be the result of pressure from either the dominant or minority group to protect what they see as their language rights. Questions of feasibility may also dictate what choices are eventually made.

Thus, although political leaders do make choices in regard to literacy issues, they nevertheless make such choices in response to a variety of external pressures. What is significant, however, is that the choices they make will ultimately affect the lives of language minority families such as the Cierras, limiting the alternatives available to them. When conflicts in agendas arise, the question of power and control becomes paramount. In such instances, typically those with the greatest power will prevail in choices regarding literacy.

What are the implications of this discussion for policymakers and educators involved in second language literacy? When formulating literacy policies in regard to immigration and nationalization regulations and the designation of a medium of instruction, policymakers and educators need to seek the ongoing involvement of the individuals and communities that will be affected by these policies. In addition, policymakers and educators need to counter the action of leaders who may limit literacy possibilities by providing inadequate funds or limited kinds of literacy education that may perpetuate existing relations of power.

In the area of immigration and naturalization policies, there are several questions that policymakers and educators should examine. First, if immigrants to Anglophone countries have a responsibility to acquire English literacy, from what basis does such responsibility arise? In addition, if they have a responsibility to become literate in English, should this extend, as it has done in the United States, to individuals seeking permanent residence, not citizenship? What is the rationale for having an English literacy requirement as opposed to a literacy requirement in any language as was done previously in the United States? If a literacy requirement is adopted, what are the responsibilities of the government to provide programs that help all individuals who wish to attain citizenship acquire the necessary literacy skills? Only when such questions are considered and debated can there be a basis for advocating particular immigration and naturalization literacy policies.

As we have seen in this chapter, the enactment of literacy campaigns in Anglophone countries has important ramifications in terms of fostering social attitudes toward literacy. First, to the extent that they focus exclusively on English literacy, they may undermine the value of literacy in other languages. Second, by depicting literacy as a problem or crisis, individuals who are not literate (in particular, not literate in English) may be viewed as a social problem. Finally, the implementation of programs designed to address the so-called literacy crisis can isolate and marginalize individuals who are not literate, particularly if one-to-one tutoring is widely used. In this way such programs can lead to feelings of inadequacy on the part of those who do not have the literacy skills deemed necessary by the campaign. Policymakers and educators then need to carefully consider the purpose that such campaigns fulfill and the ramifications of the programs included in the campaign, giving special attention to the social attitudes that such campaigns engender.

Finally, in designating the medium of instruction in public schools, policymakers and educators ought to consider the extent to which they believe public schools should develop literacy skills not just in English but also in other languages. They need to consider what benefits can ensue for Anglophone countries in promoting literacy not just in English, but in other languages as well, particularly at a time when the development of international relationships and trade is so critical to peace and economic prosperity. Perhaps most challenging, if policymakers and educators agree that promoting literacy in other languages is a priority, they should consider what kind of educational programs can be designed to meet this objective. In doing so, they will need to maintain other social priorities that the nation may have, such as a racial balance in school programs and equality of educational opportunity in order to ensure both access to programs and outcomes of learning.

Government leaders through the enactment of social policies are not the only individuals who can set second language literacy agendas. Other groups of individuals who can do so are business and labor leaders. Often they set agendas in the name of efficiency and productivity, eliciting the support of government leaders to aid in the training of a literate work force. In the next chapter, we examine second language literacy agendas that arise from economic concerns, focusing once again on the way that such decisions can determine and restrict the literacy agendas of language minorities.

3 Economic agendas for second language literacy

Melchora Galang lived in a third world country whose economy gave her very little opportunity to support herself and her family with her level of education and skills. Because of this, she decided to accept an invitation from her brother living abroad in an Anglophone country to go and live with him. Melchora was able to qualify for admission under a family preference category because her brother was a citizen of the country. It was necessary for Melchora to leave her three children with her sister, but Melchora promised to send whatever money she was able to save to her sister for the support of her children. Her brother believes that with Melchora's limited ability in spoken English, she may be able to find employment in domestic or other service work. To a large extent, Melchora's economic success or failure in her new Anglophone country depends on her ability to become literate in English.

This chapter will explore the relationships between English literacy and economic rewards in Anglophone countries that influence the ability of language minorities such as Melchora or Minh and Carlos to find work. We will discuss the role a government can play in upgrading language minorities' English literacy proficiency for employment purposes. We will also examine the manner in which a country's method of professional certification affects the ability of language minorities with professional training, such as Minh, to become certified and find employment. We will discuss the way in which literacy affects the role of language minorities in both unionized and nonunionized jobs, giving special attention to the role of women in the work force. Throughout the chapter we will view English literacy as one of several factors that affect the ability of language minorities to obtain satisfactory work. However, before examining these issues, we turn first to an examination of the role that literacy plays in the economic arena.

The role of literacy in the economic arena

Today in many developed countries the ability to process written information is viewed as the key to economic success. Stuckey (1991) maintains that the nature of work today differs from the past and that the "change, in fact, is a change *in* literacy" (p. 12). This change has resulted in what Aronowitz (1981) calls the third industrial revolution, in which the old working class has all but disappeared owing to the new demand for labor to process written information. For Stuckey, today "literacy is the language of profit," particularly in highly industrialized societies in which oral language lacks literacy's "rubber stamp." As she puts it, in the workplace today, "valid communication is written text. Valid uses of communication – i.e., profitable, legalized ones – require literacy" (p. 19).

Although Stuckey and others believe that literacy today is an important economic asset, does it in fact have economic value? Several studies suggest that in fact it does have value both for the economy as a whole and for the individual worker. One Australian study, for example, estimates that a lack of English literacy proficiency costs the commonwealth $3.2 billion per year in lower work productivity (*Business Weekly Review,* as cited in Stasiulis, 1990, p. 29). In another study, the Canadian Business Task Force of Literacy estimates that illiteracy in the workplace costs Canadian business $4.5 billion per year and Canadian society $11 billion, though these figures are considered by some to be highly speculative (Burnaby, 1991, pp. 160–161). In terms of the individual effects of literacy, recent Canadian census data shows a high correlation between low educational attainment (with presumably lower literacy proficiency) and low income level (Read & Mackay, 1984, p. 18). Research commissioned by the Adult Literacy and Basic Skills Unit in England found that adults with self-admitted literacy and numeracy problems who worked tended to be in unskilled jobs, and almost twice as many were unemployed (Adult Literacy and Basic Skills Unit, 1989, p. 4).

If English literacy today in Anglophone countries is related to profit or at least perceived so, then it would appear to be of benefit to both individual workers and employers to have a highly literate work force. However, as we shall see in this chapter, there are also benefits to having some members of the work force who are not literate in English. For example, having co-workers who are not literate makes it more likely that the literate workers will get the promotions or the better jobs. Having workers who are not literate gives employers an inexpensive labor supply for jobs that do not necessarily require literacy, such as manual labor, service work, farm work, and some assembly-line jobs.

Various interest groups can affect the complex relationship between literacy and economic rewards. Political and business leaders can sponsor workplace literacy programs for workers, increasing the likelihood that they will be able to get the better jobs that require high levels of literacy. Political and business leaders, by setting national requirements for professional certification and assessing professional knowledge in a way that requires a knowledge of English literacy practices, use literacy as a gatekeeper to determine who will benefit economically from their professional training. And finally, workers, by using unions to press for workplace literacy programs, can help determine who will develop their literacy abilities, thus contributing to their chances of getting promoted.

In considering the relationships between literacy and economic rewards, we will examine the following questions:

1. How do government leaders and employers influence the literacy training of language minorities for employment purposes both before entry to the job market and later on the job?
2. How do English literacy practices act as a gatekeeper for both the passing of professional certification examinations and the gaining of influence in labor unions?
3. What are the implications of not being literate for finding work?

Throughout this chapter it is assumed that English literacy is a necessary but by no means sufficient condition for economic advancement in Anglophone countries. Factors such as race and gender play a critical role in hiring practices even though employers may point to a lack of English literacy as the central determining factor in hiring. In so doing, employers suggest that responsibility for not getting a job rests in the individual and his or her lack of English literacy rather than in larger social and economic factors, when in reality such factors are critical in employment. We turn now to an examination of how governments themselves can strive to increase the productivity of the country by funding programs that develop literacy and job-related skills.

Government-sponsored job training for language minorities

In many Anglophone countries today, the economic costs of not having a literate society are being emphasized. Lo Bianco (1989), for example, in reference to Australia, notes the current attention being given to the economic value of furthering adult literacy, typically phrased exclusively in terms of English literacy. As he points out:

Recently, much more attention has been paid to the economic costs to the nation of allowing significant numbers of adults to remain "incommunicado" in the society's most powerful symbolic system for storing and conveying knowledge. . . . No longer is literacy of peripheral concern but it is now an important corollary of labour market programs, of economic restructuring, of the adaptability, mobility and more highly skilled type of work force for the "productive culture" which economic prescriptions of Australia argue is essential. (p. viii)

As was noted in Chapter 2, one alternative that governments can undertake to try to attain a highly literate work force is to sponsor literacy campaigns. A second alternative is to fund job-training programs that include a literacy component. One country that is actively pursuing this alternative is Canada. In order to illustrate some of the barriers that exist in undertaking a successful national literacy job-training program, we turn to an examination of Canada's job-training program with specific attention to the training programs available to the immigrant population.

Canadian language training programs for immigrants

In Canada, the division of labor between the federal and provincial governments in reference to literacy training and education is not clear-cut. Whereas the provinces have exclusive jurisdiction over matters of education, the federal government has responsibility for training. Thus, language programs for immigrants specifically related to work are a federal responsibility administered by the Commission for Employment and Immigration (CEIC) (Read & Mackay, 1984, p. 61). Not all immigrants, however, are eligible for federally sponsored language training related to work.

Eligibility depends both on the category under which an immigrant is admitted and the policies surrounding his or her admission. According to Read and Mackay (1984), Canada's immigration policy "attempts to reconcile various 'immigration imperatives' among which are: respect for the family, response to domestic manpower demands and humanitarian concerns" (pp. 61–62). In order to best meet domestic employment needs, Canada is highly selective in admitting potential immigrants by use of a points scheme. Under this scheme, points are awarded to individuals wishing to immigrate according to their practical experience, previous job training, official language ability, previous education, and age. To ensure that immigrants accepted into Canada possess work skills that are in demand, employment-related factors account for almost half of the total possible points. In this way individuals who have a high level of education, specific vocational preparation, and occupational experience, particularly in occupations where there is a demand for workers, are awarded a high number of points for admission.

According to Read and Mackay (1984), this policy is seen as "being in the best interests of both Canada's economic welfare and the immigrants' personal welfare since it increases the likelihood that appropriate and gainful employment is quickly found" (p. 62). Under this policy, immigrants such as Minh would gain points for their previous occupational and educational training. If, however, their occupational field were not currently in demand in the economy, they would not receive many points in that area. Immigrants such as Carlos, on the other hand, because they are not highly trained workers, would likely have few points awarded for entry. Finally, immigrants such as Melchora, although gaining no points for previous training, would get some points because of their knowledge of English. Such a point system affects the makeup of the immigrant work force. Underlying the implementation of such a system can be a hidden agenda. For example, in the medical profession, few points are awarded in the area of professional demand. In this way, the assigning of demand points can protect Canadians whose jobs could be jeopardized by an influx of immigrants in their field. As we shall see shortly, even when immigrants with professional training are allowed entry, however, they often are not allowed to practice their profession until they have passed professional certification examinations. It is in this endeavor that knowledge of English literacy practices will play a central role.

Not all immigrants to Canada, however, are assessed on the point system. Of the three main classes of immigrants admitted to Canada – "family class," "Convention refugees," and "independent" – only certain applicants coming in under the independent classification are assessed under the point system. On the other hand, immigrants from any of the three classes who are destined for the work force are eligible for language training under CEIC if they need additional language skills to obtain a job, but in practice not all applicants have an equal chance of getting job training or the subsistence allowance that may accompany it. Whereas some immigrants coming in under the independent and refugee classification are eligible for both full-time language training and subsistence allowances while they are studying, immigrants coming in under the family class usually do not receive subsistence allowances because their sponsors have financial responsibility for them. One effect of this policy is that because most women enter Canada under the family class, few are eligible for a subsistence allowance during their language training (Read & Mackay, 1984, pp. 63–64).

Furthermore, many immigrant women do not receive full-time language training even though they lack language abilities in French or English. Some immigrant women do not get this language training because they are not destined directly for the work force, a criterion that applicants must meet to qualify for the language training. More significant, it has been common practice for employment center counselors to refer only one member of the family to language training, usually the male (Canada Employment and Immigration Advisory Council, 1991, p. 8). In addition, of the women destined directly for the work force, many find jobs in spite of their lack of English or French and take jobs as garment workers, dishwashers, or hotel workers, in which their lack of mastery of an official language is not critical. The problem, however, is that "without official language and literacy skills, they may be trapped in these occupational ghettos – having to work but unable to gain official language facility, upgrade their skills and therefore be unable to get a better job" (Read & Mackay, 1984, p. 64). The system, then, as it now operates makes the woman immigrant worker one of the least likely to attain full-time government language training or a subsistence allowance and thus one of the least likely to reap the possible economic benefits that can arise from more developed language and literacy abilities. [In fact, in 1988 almost 61 percent of female immigrants were not eligible for language training as compared to only 12 percent of males (Canada Employment and Immigration Advisory Council, 1991, p. 5).]

CEIC provides language training opportunities for adult immigrants through three main programs. The largest of these is for immigrants who are immediately destined for the work force and involves the purchase of classroom language-training programs by the federal government from provincial community colleges and private institutions. Under this program eligible immigrants may receive up to thirty weeks of full-time language instruction at a community college or private institution. The second program, the Language at Work (LAW) program, is a work-based program for immigrant language training. It provides funds to employers to initiate in-house language programs. The final program, the Settlement Language Program (SLP), is aimed at persons not immediately destined for the labor force, particularly immigrant women. These language programs usually include on-site baby-sitting and provide transportation services where necessary. All of these programs are aimed at upgrading the language and literacy proficiency of immigrants, thus increasing their chances of getting a better job. However, several problems undermine the successful implementation of the programs.

According to a report issued by the Canada Employment and Immigration Advisory Council entitled *Immigrants and Language Training* (1991, p. 53), one of the major problems facing language programs for immigrants has to do with the many levels of bureaucracy responsible for administering the programs. Because training is a federal responsibility whereas education is a provincial responsibility, language-training program funds pass through several layers of bureaucracy before actual instruction is delivered. These layers include federal officials, provincial ministers, and institutional administrators. These many levels of authority make responsibility and accountability very difficult to achieve, resulting in programs in which there are no standards as to course design, duration of training, or teacher qualification. In fact, in many instances teachers are not trained in the field. According to the council's report, "a cohesive and national language program is currently nonexistent because of this confusing splintering of essential services for immigrant settlement at both the federal and provincial levels" (p. 54).

Although the Canadian government has assumed a responsibility for language training for its immigrant population, its efforts to develop the language and literacy abilities of immigrants for work-related purposes are being undermined by the bureaucracy that surrounds the programs. Conflicting agendas between various levels of bureaucracy interfere with the implementation of the training, resulting in programs that are not fully satisfactory. In addition, the regulations regarding eligibility for the programs affect the immigrant population in unequal ways. As the programs now exist, women are less likely to attend them and thus reap the possible economic benefits of increased language and literacy skills. Women such as Melchora would have less chance to qualify for both full-time language training and a subsistence allowance than would their male counterparts. The situation of immigrant women in the work force is one that warrants attention in many Anglophone countries. Not only do women often have less access to job training, but, as we shall see, they are often discriminated against in hiring practices and union activities.

Recognition of overseas qualifications

Government-sponsored job training programs that involve language training are only one way a government can influence the relationship between literacy proficiency and economic rewards. Government and business leaders also have an effect on this relationship through the establishment of professional certification requirements. In many Anglophone countries, when workers such as Minh, who have professional skills, want to get a job, they must first get their overseas training recognized through some type of qualification procedure. In order to illustrate the effect of these requirements on the ability of workers such as Minh to benefit economically from their professional training, we will examine the certification procedures of Australia, which has a large number of immigrants with overseas professional training.

Australian overseas skills recognition

The immigrant population of Australia is exceptionally large; in fact, Australia has a larger percentage of its population born overseas than any other developed country except for Israel. Furthermore, the skill level of the immigrant population is consistently higher, on average, than that of the Australian-born work force (Stasiulis, 1990, pp. 32–33). However, many overseas-educated immigrants are not able to work in the profession in which they were trained, resulting in a significant economic loss to the country. Although there are no comprehensive statistics available on the number of immigrants who cannot have their vocational skills recognized and thus never return to their previous occupations, commonwealth policy documents contend that "the annual loss from the wasted community investment in overseas skills is estimated to be in the order of $100 million to $350 million" (Stasiulis, 1990, pp. 33–34). What prevents immigrants such as Minh who wish to return to their former profession from doing so, thus contributing to the Australian economy as a whole?

One of the major barriers is the current Australian certification procedures. In his investigation of overseas skill recognition, Stasiulis (1990) points out that Australia, compared with many other industrial-

ized societies, has a highly regulated labor market. Although the official reasons given for such regulations are the need to safeguard public
health and safety and to guarantee high standards of work, another
reason that is operative is "the desire of occupational groups to protect
their earnings, working conditions, and frequently their exclusiveness"
(p. 36). As with the point system in Canada, Australian certification
procedures can be used by those with jobs to protect their jobs. Hence,
although the economy of the country may benefit from utilizing the
skills of overseas-trained workers, those who currently hold such jobs
want to protect their own interests.

According to Stasiulis (1990), three areas of the current certification
process present special problems for immigrants such as Minh who
hope to return to their premigration occupations. These problems have
to do with the recognition system itself, with the information and
counseling services available to overseas-trained immigrants, and finally,
with inadequate retraining courses. Problems arising in each of these
areas undermine the chances for immigrants such as Minh to benefit
economically from their professional training. In all instances, the
English literacy practices used in the certification process serve as a
gatekeeper in determining who will be certified.

Currently in Australia, in order to be recognized in a profession,
immigrants must deal with a wide range of registration, licensing, and
certification procedures that are administered by federal and state
governments as well as by trade and professional bodies and employers. Furthermore, many of the recognition processes require a
considerable length of time, with some applications taking up to a year.
During these waiting periods, immigrants such as Minh are either
unemployed or employed in jobs that do not utilize their skills. Furthermore, in some cases certification requirements are not uniformly
applied so that those who are not trained in a system developed from a
British model must undergo additional testing. In this way, "education
and training in British-style programs . . . become the grounds for
recognition, rather than occupational competence" (Stasiulis, 1990,
p. 40). Regardless of where they were trained, however, in order to be
certified all nonnative speakers of English face some type of evaluation of their English language abilities. This can occur directly through
an English test or as part of an oral or written test of professional
content.

Much criticism has been leveled at all of the procedures for testing
English, with critics pointing out that the level of English required for
some professions is unrealistically high and often used as a tool of

discrimination (Stasiulis, 1990, p. 42). In order, then, for immigrants such as Minh to gain professional recognition, they will need to have their professional knowledge formally certified through some type of testing procedure, as well as demonstrate a certain level of English proficiency, one that may be set unnecessarily high. In passing these exams, they will need to get information regarding testing and registration procedures, information that may be particularly difficult for nonnative speakers of English to obtain.

Stasiulis (1990) points out that many immigrants arrive in Australia with "very little understanding of why they must have their qualifications 'recognized' and with even less knowledge and understanding of how to go about it" (p. 44). Frequently immigration officials, not knowing about procedures for certification, convey a good deal of misinformation to immigrants. In general, then, immigrants are given little information about how the system works and "how to navigate these systems" (p. 44). Such problems illustrate the manner in which gaining access to the job market requires not merely knowing the language but also knowing how the language operates within a whole structure of discourse. In this way, literacy, as was pointed out in Chapter 1, cannot be separated from social practices. As Gee (1990) says:

Literacy practices are almost always fully integrated with, interwoven into, constitute part of, the very texture of the wider practices that involve talk, interaction, values and beliefs. You can no more cut the literacy out of the overall social practice, or cut away the non-literacy parts from the literacy parts of the overall practice, than you can subtract the white squares from a chess board and still have a chess board. (p. 43)

By not having knowledge of the complex social practices of which English literacy is a part, immigrants such as Minh, even if they have a good grasp of the structure and vocabulary of the language, are less likely to pass the certification requirements and thus receive some of the economic benefits that can accompany their professional training.

Finally, Australian immigrants in trying to achieve professional recognition also experience problems in the so-called bridging programs that are available. Such programs serve one of three purposes: They prepare professionals for exams, they act as an accreditation vehicle in that passing the course certifies the individual, or they are part of a regular final year of a graduate program that overseas professionals can attend to gain recognition. One of the major problems immigrants face involves a lack of knowledge regarding culture-specific forms of testing (Stasiulis, 1990, pp. 46–47). Many immigrants are not familiar with the multiple-choice exam form, which is commonly used in Australia, and because of this have problems passing the tests. Once again, by not being familiar with the social practices in which English literacy is embedded, immigrants such as Minh are less likely to get certified and reap the economic benefits of their professional knowledge.

Immigrants such as Minh face a series of obstacles in attaining their own personal agenda of getting work compatible with their skills. Being able to read and write English is a necessary but by no means sufficient condition for them to obtain employment. In addition to having knowledge of English and a professional field, they must learn the complex set of social practices of which literacy is a part so that they will be able to deal with the bureaucratic forms, tests, and interviews that provide entry to a new job. English literacy practices, then, serve as a gatekeeper in the Australian certification procedure, a process that will determine who will and who will not reap the possible economic benefits of professional knowledge. A similar situation exists in Canada, where it was found that 31 percent of immigrants had not found a job in their intended occupation after three years of residence in the country. The main reasons that respondents cited for this fact were language deficiencies, lack of Canadian experience, and not having their qualifications accepted by professional or trade associations (Read & Mackay, 1984, p. 105).

Although being familiar with English literacy practices is a necessary but by no means sufficient condition for attaining one of the better jobs, not having any English literacy abilities ensures that immigrants will not get the more desirable jobs. In being restricted from securing one of the better jobs, such immigrants play an important role in the overall health of the economy of a country. We turn now to a discussion of the role that unskilled immigrants who are not literate in English can play in the economy of Anglophone countries.

Language minorities in the unskilled and nonunionized labor market

When Carlos first entered the country without legal papers, he was willing to take any job that would provide money for his family back home. Like many undocumented workers, he was able to find work in an unskilled, nonunion position in agriculture. In light of what

Aronowitz (1981) calls the third industrial revolution of highly developed countries – in which the old working class has all but disappeared – what role does a language minority such as Carlos play in the labor market?

Unskilled and nonunionized workers in the United States

In analyzing the role of alien workers in Western Europe, Skutnabb-Kangas (1981) contends that such workers serve as a buffer between the native-born population and downturns in the economy because they generally are the last hired and first fired. In examining the role of undocumented workers in the United States, Spener (1988, p. 139) maintains that such individuals in the United States serve a similar but somewhat different purpose. He contends that undocumented workers in the United States are necessary for the thousands of "bad" jobs, or what economists call jobs in the secondary labor market, that exist in the economy. The type of work that constitutes one of these jobs is not necessarily different from that of a good job. The difference lies in the fact that a less desirable job does not pay a worker an adequate living wage. Nor do jobs in the secondary labor market provide health benefits, convenient hours, or safe working conditions. A unionized unskilled job in itself may be no better or worse than any other type of unskilled job. The difference is that unionized workers can have a better job because they can organize and press for certain working conditions.

Spener (1988, p. 139) argues that there is no shortage of unskilled labor in the United States; rather, there is a shortage of workers who are willing to take jobs in the secondary labor market. He believes that the role of undocumented workers, particularly in farm labor jobs, is to fill these less desirable jobs. Support for this position is evident in the rhetoric surrounding the passage of the U.S. Immigration Reform and Control Act (IRCA), the agricultural amnesty program, referred to in Chapter 2. Thompson and Martin (1991) point out that during the legislative debates surrounding the passage of the IRCA, agricultural employers expressed the concern that agricultural workers with their newly gained legal resident status and "no restraints on where they could hold jobs, would quit field jobs in agriculture for higher wages and less seasonal nonfarm work" (p. 529). If a shortage of workers did materialize, the growers argued, they would need access "to supplemental foreign workers as insurance against production losses" (p. 530). In response to this concern, the Replenishment Agricultural

Worker program, a guest-worker program involving many workers who were already in the United States without official work authorization, was established to provide replacement workers. Thus, although it would seem that a country's productivity is best served by having a highly literate work force, in fact there are agendas that are served by having workers who are willing to take the less desirable jobs. Often these workers are individuals such as Carlos who are not literate in English and thus do not have access to the better jobs.

Ogbu and Matute-Bianchi (1986) offer another way of explaining why language minorities are willing to take jobs in the secondary labor market. Ogbu describes what he calls castelike minorities in the United States. These are people who were originally brought into the United States involuntarily through slavery, conquest, or colonization. American Indians and black Americans are two examples of this group. Often these individuals are perceived by the dominant group to be inherently inferior in all aspects of intelligence and ability to carry out the high-level skills demanded of jobs with prestige.

He contrasts this with immigrant minorities who have moved more or less voluntarily to the United States for better economic opportunities or greater political freedom. Although these people may be treated in much the same way as castelike minorities by the dominant group, they respond differently to the situation. Because many immigrants in this group come to their new country to improve their economic condition, they measure their success not in reference to the dominant group but rather in reference to the situation from which they came. In Ogbu and Matute-Bianchi's perspective, immigrants such as Carlos and Melchora, who left to improve their economic lot, may view any improvement in their economic condition as success and be willing to accept discrimination as a necessary condition for their economic improvement. Although their lack of knowledge of English literacy practices limits their ability to get the better jobs, they are willing to take jobs in the secondary labor market because they view such jobs in relation to their previous economic conditions.

Women in the unskilled and nonunionized labor market

In many countries, immigrant women such as Melchora form a large proportion of the work force in some of the least desirable jobs. This is particularly true of immigrant women who are not literate. For example, in a study of illiterate adult immigrants in Canada, Read and Mackay (1984, p. 52) found that half of the illiterate immigrant women workers in their survey worked in two of the lowest-paying sectors of the Canadian work force, namely the service occupations (working as baby-sitters, domestic help, dishwashers, office cleaners, and hotel workers) and the fabric industries. One-third of all immigrant women, whether literate or illiterate, worked in these two fields compared with one-fifth of all women workers. Many of these immigrant women worked in the product-fabricating and product-assembling occupations as sewing machine operators and assembly-line workers, where working conditions have been described as "horrendous," the speed "frantic," and the pay "meager" (Read & Mackay, 1984, p. 53). In Canada, as is the case in many other countries, such poor working conditions are prevalent in the low-paying jobs in which unskilled immigrant women workers are typically employed. Often women such as Melchora receive little pay because many work as seasonal farm workers and domestic help in which minimum wage legislation may not apply or is not enforced (Read & Mackay, 1984, p. 104). This situation illustrates once again the difficult plight of immigrant women, particularly those who do not have the literacy abilities deemed necessary for the better jobs.

Language minorities in the unionized labor market

One way in which workers can exert pressure for such things as better working conditions, literacy classes, and job skill training is through unions. Although many immigrants do have union jobs, as we shall see, a good many factors operate within unions that can work to reduce the pressure of people such as Carlos and Melchora to meet their on-the-job needs. In order to understand why this is so, we turn now to a discussion of the role of language minorities in unionized jobs, focusing specifically on Australia, a country in which immigrants are highly unionized. In fact, Australian foreign-born workers are more unionized than their Australian counterparts (Stasiulis, 1990, p. 79).

The role of Australian immigrants in labor unions

Although many Australian foreign-born workers belong to unions, unions appear to be doing little to meet the special needs of the immigrant population, frequently because immigrants themselves are not able to promote their own interests. According to Stasiulis (1990,

p. 23), several factors undermine the ability of immigrants from non–English-speaking countries to press for their concerns through union activities. First of all, many language minorities are caught in a vicious circle in which their poor English makes it difficult for them to influence union actions that could result in workplace literacy programs, which in turn might improve their communication skills and thus enable them to participate more actively in the union. A second factor that may account for the lack of union response to the needs of foreign-born workers is racism. In early Australian unionism, union policies were concerned with preserving the "whiteness" of Australia by immigration restrictions and work bans on Asian settlers. More recently, racism has been evident in many union members' concern about the increased number of immigrant workers, many of whom are nonwhite. Some union members argue that such workers will depress wages, create unemployment, and increase pressure on present shortages such as housing (Stasiulis, 1990, p. 78).

A final factor that makes it difficult for foreign-born workers to gain influential posts in unions and thus lobby for their interests has to do with the centralized organization of unions in Australia. Because, in general, unions in Australia do not encourage rank-and-file involvement except at occasional mass meetings, the primary way in which foreign-born workers can make an impact on union activities is to gain leadership roles. However, because of their lack of English and because of racism, this is difficult to do. Hence, foreign-born workers, even though unionized, tend to have little impact on getting the union to meet their particular needs. There are, in addition, a variety of factors that keep women particularly from being active in union activities. These include "family and childcare responsibilities and lack of childcare provisions, the double day of work, inconvenient union meeting times, sexism of male union officials and gender-specific English language difficulties" (Stasiulis, 1990, p. 81).

All of this is occurring during a period in which many immigrant workers in Australia are losing their jobs. Currently in Australia, there is a move to restructure labor in order to make the labor market more flexible and thus increase Australia's competitiveness in the international market. This restructuring involves such actions as reducing occupational classifications in order to improve productivity and efficiency. Many of the key industries targeted for such restructuring have a high concentration of workers from non–English-speaking countries, many of whom are older, with low or unrecognized trade skills and with insufficient English literacy abilities to allow them to participate in training and career development (Stasiulis, 1990, p. 21). Because of this fact, the restructuring process has taken place at the expense of the immigrant workers. For example, one of the industrial sectors that experienced heavy job losses because of restructuring was the textile, clothing, and footwear industries, whose work force is composed primarily of language minority women (Stasiulis, 1990, p. 21). In Australia, as in the agricultural sector of the United States, immigrant workers such as Carlos and Melchora are acting as buffers and losing their jobs when the economy warrants. One of the reasons for this is their lack of English language and literacy abilities, which prevents them from being effective champions of their own work-related concerns.

For immigrants such as Carlos and Melchora various factors undermine their ability to influence unions to protect their jobs and to press for their particular literacy needs. In many cases, however, employers themselves are becoming concerned about the limited literacy abilities of their workers, believing that low-level literacy abilities diminish the productivity of the company. Because of this, they are setting up various types of workplace literacy programs. In order to understand the various agendas that can operate in the development of workplace literacy programs, we turn now to a discussion of such programs.

Workplace literacy

Problems in implementation

In some countries, workplace literacy programs are given a high priority because of the economic costs of having a work force that is not literate. Australia, for one, has placed workplace literacy high on the national agenda. One problem that exists in implementing such programs, however, has to do with funding: Should workplace literacy programs be sponsored by the government or by private industry? In Australia the government has decided, by and large, not to fund such programs directly. In fact, within the total government Adult Migrant Education Program (AMEP) budget of $71.572 million, only a negligible percentage of that budget (one quarter of a million) was allocated for English in the Workplace (Stasiulis, 1990, p. 26). The rationale for this was that such funds were intended to be used as a catalyst for industry itself to fund English programs in the workplace.

However, many issues in both union and employer circles in Australia are reducing the likelihood that industry will sponsor such workplace literacy programs. Although the Australian Council of Trade Unions (ACTU) has urged its state branches to actively campaign for paid-leave English-language and literacy training and has been successful in achieving some programs, such initiatives are being resisted by both employers and unions (Stasiulis, 1990, p. 24). Employers, in some instances, are pulling workers out of English-language and literacy training classes whenever the workers are needed to meet increased production demands, thus decreasing the effectiveness of the programs' impact. At the same time, several unions are ambivalent about the inclusion of English in the workplace and about release time for such courses. This is primarily because the co-workers of language minority workers are often openly hostile to the idea of language minority workers getting what they see as "preferential treatment" and a "paid holiday" (Stasiulis, 1990, p. 27).

The language minority workers in turn are afraid of their co-workers' hostility. In fact, in one study of the New South Wales State Rail and Urban Transit Authorities, 55 percent of language minority workers expressed fear that their co-workers would complain about their taking English workplace courses, viewing it as special treatment (Palmer, 1984, as cited in Stasiulis, 1990, p. 27). Perhaps because of the pervasiveness of such feelings, both trade union officials and members of some large unions are opposed to special privileges being granted to specific groups of workers in the form of paid leave for English-language and literacy training (Stasiulis, 1990, p. 27). Problems in the implementation of workplace literacy programs, then, arise from funding issues and from lack of support among employers and workers.

Another problem that often occurs in the implementation of workplace literacy programs is the question of who should control the design of the course. Management may have its own set of agendas for workplace programs, often those of helping the industry run more efficiently. If management is the funding source, then it has a great deal of power in the design of a literacy program. It may believe that only objectives that meet the direct learning needs of industry should be addressed. Furthermore, it may fear that if learners increase their literacy abilities, they will become more active in the union or quit their job for a better one. [In fact, Read and Mackay (1984, p. 125) point out that in Canada, many workplace courses were stopped for just such reasons.] On the other hand, employees may have literacy needs regarding such issues as legalization, certification requirements, or job mobility, which go beyond the scope of management's expectations for literacy.

Not only the content but also the schedule is an issue that surrounds workplace literacy programs. Often management is reluctant to incorporate a course into regular work hours because of the costs involved. In addition, co-workers, as has been pointed out, can feel that some workers are getting preferential treatment if they are paid for literacy instruction. On the other hand, if employees are asked to take a course after work hours, the additional hours may be quite difficult to manage owing to family and personal needs.

The conflicts surrounding the question of whether or not literacy training should be part of the work day was highlighted in a Canadian report by the National Advisory Panel on Skill Development Leave. In its final report, the committee recommended paid educational leaves for workers but included the reservation that no more than 2 percent of the work force from any one industry should be absent on literacy leave at any one time. This in effect means that in those industries in which there are a large number of immigrant women needing literacy training, only a small proportion can take advantage of the program. Furthermore, in order for group instruction to take place and be financially feasible, the industry would have to be very large to implement a paid educational leave program (Read & Mackay 1984, p. 66). The recommendation of the committee represents a compromise that tries to meet both workers' literacy needs and employers' concern with cost. It reflects the power conflict that underlies many workplace literacy programs. As Read and Mackay (1984) point out, "workplace classes always face a double dilemma. Whose interests do they serve and who pays?" (p. 67). Such conflicts, as we have seen, undermine the implementation of workplace literacy programs and can reduce the possibility that these programs will meet the personal literacy agendas of workers such as Carlos and Melchora.

Union-initiated workplace literacy programs

In light of the possible conflict between employers' and workers' interests in implementing workplace literacy programs, several unions in the United States are currently pressing for workplace literacy programs designed by unions and jointly funded by unions and employers. The rationale for such an approach is elaborated in a report done by Sarmiento and Kay (1990), sponsored by the largest U.S.

association of unions, the AFL-CIO (American Federation of Labor and Congress of Industrial Organizations). Sarmiento and Kay (1990) argue that because unions represent the potential learners, they are in a unique position to look after their interests in education. Furthermore, they maintain that other educational programs cannot adequately deal with the education and literacy needs of workers. Public schools, they argue, cannot handle the vast needs of workers in a changing workplace; furthermore, three quarters of the people who will be working in the year 2000 are now out of school. Existing adult education programs are generally oriented to traditional high school curricula and so are not able to meet the particular needs of workers. Volunteer-based literacy programs, too, are inadequate because most are underfunded and unfamiliar with education and training for the workplace. In contrast, programs based in the workplace have the advantage of having learners who share similar job experiences and needs (Sarmiento & Kay, 1990, p. 14).

According to Sarmiento and Kay, union-sponsored training programs that include literacy classes can achieve the following workplace objectives. First, they can protect union members' employment security. In one instance, when bus drivers had to face a new driver's license test to keep their jobs, the union program helped the members prepare for the test. Second, such programs can increase the members' job advancement opportunities and help advance the safety and health of workers. And finally, they can respond to the members' personal interests and education so that such things as citizenship courses can be a component of the course (Sarmiento & Kay, 1990, pp. 11–12). Certainly, many of these objectives would help immigrants such as Carlos and Melchora to maintain their jobs, get promoted, and meet their larger literacy needs. The problem is that their chances of being able to participate in such programs are very small, particularly if such a program is funded, at least in part, by the employer.

Sarmiento and Kay (1990, p. 22) point out that today in the United States, it is estimated that only one employee in ten receives formal training of any kind from his or her employer, with employers spending only 1.4 percent of the national payroll on training. In addition, with few exceptions, most employers concentrate their paid training on the managerial elite so that college graduates have a 50 percent greater probability of getting training on the job than do high school graduates. In general, the less formal education one has, the less likely an employer will invest in this individual's training or education. What this suggests, of course, is that workers such as Carlos and Melchora would be highly unlikely to receive literacy training that was funded even in part by the employer.

What should be included in workplace literacy programs

In implementing workplace literacy programs, one critical issue has to do with the content of the program. The two most prevalent models for workplace literacy programs are what Wrigley (as cited in Isserlis, 1991, p. 1) terms workplace-specific programs and workplace-general programs. In the former type of program, only the language and literacy practices needed for specific jobs at a specific site are dealt with. In workplace-general programs, on the other hand, more general employment skills (e.g., seeking clarification, complaining about unfair treatment, or dealing with cross-cultural communication problems may be part of the program.

Even though most employers prefer the workplace-specific model, there are persuasive reasons for selecting the latter, particularly in the case of language minority workers. In order to understand this, it is helpful to examine several components of literacy as a social practice. Reder (1987) contends that whereas some literacy activities (such as reading a book) can be individual endeavors, often literacy activities occur in a social context and are collaborative efforts. For example, in a workplace context, a "boss" (one social role in a literacy practice) may dictate a letter to a "secretary" (another social role in the literacy practice). "The fact that the secretary rather than the boss is doing the actual writing (i.e. functions as the 'scribe') may or may not reflect the distribution of specialized literacy skills between the two; more likely it reflects their relative statuses within the organization in which they work" (p. 256).

√ For Reder (1987) when literacy is a collaborative undertaking, three modes of engagement are possible. The first is *technological engagement,* in which an individual is engaged in the actual technology of writing or reading. The second is *functional engagement,* in which an individual supplies knowledge or expertise necessary for the enactment of the literacy practice. Finally, there is *social engagement,* in which, individuals – although not necessarily technologically or functionally engaged – have a knowledge of the nature of the practice and its implications for the community.

Reder gives an example of how these levels of engagement interacted in the case of a town meeting he attended. In this situation, one individual took on the task of writing a formal letter (technological engagement). Another individual, who could not write a formal letter himself, nevertheless had the political savvy to understand how to use the letter to write to the editor of a regional newspaper in order to advance the town's interest (functional engagement). And finally, a third individual, a town elder, had the historical knowledge to provide the relevant background information necessary to compose a persuasive letter (social engagement).

Reder contends that each of these three components of collaborative literacy is learned as a practice. In some instances, an individual may have knowledge of one type of engagement, but he or she may not be knowledgeable of another. For example, although a language minority worker may know how to write a letter of request for paid literacy training (technological engagement), he or she may not know how to use the letter effectively in a workplace to get a favorable response to the request (functional engagement). Furthermore, the worker may not have the necessary background knowledge of the situation to couch the request in a manner that will ensure a favorable response (social engagement).

In order for language minorities to be able to successfully use literacy practices to promote their own literacy agendas in the workplace, they need to be able to handle all three levels of engagement. However, because of their unfamiliarity with the culture, language minorities often lack ability in the area of functional and social engagement. Whereas workplace-specific programs tend to deal primarily with technological engagement, workplace-general programs at least provide the possibility of helping workers gain knowledge of the other levels of engagement. This knowledge is important for them to have in order to promote their own literacy agendas. For example, in order for Carlos to get amnesty literacy issues dealt with as part of a workplace literacy program, it would be of great benefit for him to have the functional and social knowledge necessary to write a letter of request on this matter to his employer or union. In the same way, if Melchora had such knowledge she might be able to press for literacy training that would go beyond the specific needs of her job to more general literacy training that might result in a promotion.

The problem, however, is that employers, as has been noted, may not support workplace-general literacy programs, viewing them as a waste of time and resources which will not benefit the company overall. On the other hand, unless programs deal with literacy as a social practice, language minorities will have less opportunity to attain some of their own literacy agendas, possibly increasing their chances of reaping the economic benefits of literacy. How this conflict is resolved will ultimately depend on who controls the programs and whose interest they serve. Very often, as in the political arena, individuals such as Melchora and Carlos, who have less power, have less chance of having their literacy agendas met.

Summary and implications

In this chapter we have examined several conflicting agendas regarding literacy in the economic arena. Viewing literacy as an economic asset, government leaders and employers are often anxious to promote job-related literacy training. However, the enactment of such programs can be undermined by competing agendas. As we have seen in the case of Canadian language programs, conflicts between various levels of bureaucracy can minimize the effectiveness of job-related literacy programs. In many industry-sponsored workplace literacy programs, employers and employees can have different agendas regarding the ultimate goals of the programs. Whereas employers often see the goal of such programs as developing highly specialized literacy practices with immediate applicability to specific jobs, workers may want to develop more general literacy practices, some of which could lead them to pursue other worker interests or to seek alternate jobs.

We have also explored various arenas that affect the relationship between literacy and economic rewards. In the area of professional certification, English literacy practices serve a gatekeeper function in determining who will or will not be able to use their professional knowledge for getting one of the better jobs. Government-sponsored language training can develop English literacy abilities, thus increasing the likelihood that the participants of the program will get jobs. Finally, labor unions can exert pressure on employers to sponsor workplace literacy programs, thus increasing the likelihood of job promotion for participants.

Finally, we have examined the role of literacy in gaining access to the job market. Today many jobs, particularly the good ones, demand high levels of literacy abilities to process information. In order to acquire this knowledge, one must have the opportunity to enroll in programs that upgrade job skills, a task that is often difficult for language minorities because of government bureaucracy. When individuals are not able to develop their literacy abilities, they are often relegated to the less desirable jobs of the country. Ironically, they can be beneficial to the country by acting as an economic buffer, being the first to be let go when economic conditions warrant a cutback.

Many factors can serve to undermine the ability of workers such as Minh, Carlos, and Melchora to develop the literacy practices needed to get one of the more desirable jobs through government job-training programs or workplace literacy classes. Also undermined is their ability to reap the economic benefits of those professional skills they already have by becoming certified by the state. Such issues as professional certification procedures, requirements for eligibility for job training programs, and unfamiliarity with the social practices surrounding bureaucratic structures and labor unions all serve to reduce their chances of obtaining one of the better jobs.

What are the implications of this situation for second language literacy educators and policymakers? First, in reference to government-sponsored literacy training and professional certification requirements, it is likely that a good deal of bureaucracy will be involved in their implementation. Although there may be little that can be done to eliminate such bureaucracy, policymakers can strive to provide mechanisms for language minorities, many of whom are unfamiliar with the complex layers of bureaucracy, to find help in dealing with it. Unless language minorities are provided with such help, they will be denied opportunities to further their job and literacy training and to demonstrate their professional and literacy abilities – both necessary steps in increasing the possibility of securing a better job. In addition, policymakers need to establish procedures to ensure that both government-sponsored literacy training and professional certification requirements are fairly applied, working to eliminate gender and ethnic discrimination in their implementation.

With regard to the workplace itself, policymakers can strive to provide incentives for industry to establish on-site, release time programs for language minorities, recognizing that in many Anglophone countries, language minorities will constitute an ever-increasing percentage of the work force. To the extent that increased literacy abilities contribute to work productivity and job satisfaction, it is to the benefit of industry to support literacy programs. Second language educators involved in workplace literacy programs need to develop curricula that deal not just with workplace-specific but also with workplace-general literacy and the social practices that surround literacy. Only by learning these social practices will language minorities be able to use their literacy abilities for their own benefit.

Finally, second language literacy educators need to carefully consider the kind of workplace orientation they wish to promote in their classrooms. As we have seen, many factors in society at large result in language minorities' having the least desirable jobs. If literacy curricula foster images of language minorities working in the less desirable jobs, they can promote and reinforce social attitudes about the role of language minorities in the work force. In addition, it is important for educators to realize that, although mastering literacy as it operates in the workplace may be an important goal for language minorities, these individuals may have other literacy agendas that are equally or more important to them. Some of these may arise from their personal and family lives.

In the next chapter we will examine some of these personal agendas. We will explore how family members can set literacy agendas for one another and how the family provides a learning environment for literacy practices, both in the first and second languages. In addition, we will consider the ways in which political leaders, researchers, and educators have depicted the role of language minority families in the development of literacy.

4 Family agendas for second language literacy

Both the Tran and the Cierra families have a good deal of printed material in their homes. In their mother tongue they have articles such as letters from friends, religious books, and newsletters; in English there are such items as instructions on medicine, directions on food products, school bulletins, and government forms. These printed materials often form the basis for family interactions in which the parents and children share their knowledge of English and their mother tongue to talk about the printed materials. The interactions that occur around these items are examples of family literacy practices. When the children in the family enter school, they will be asked to become involved in school literacy practices. The manner in which these family and school literacy experiences affect one another is one focus of this chapter.

When family members interact around the printed word, they can often set literacy agendas for one another. When children bring into the home printed items from school, parents may have to deal with these materials. If the parents are not able to read such items, they may seek help from friends and relatives, or they may be embarrassed by their lack of English ability and avoid dealing with the item altogether, or they may decide to increase their proficiency in English in order to deal with such things in the future. In any case, the children by their involvement in school have set a literacy agenda for their parents. On the other hand, parents can also set agendas for their children. They may encourage their children to read to them or to complete written school assignments at home. If they are not literate themselves, they may ask their children to act as interpreters for them. In such instances the parents set literacy agendas for their children. These examples illustrate the manner in which family members can set literacy agendas for each other. This type of agenda setting is another focus of this chapter.

In addition, outside forces can set agendas for language minority families. In the previous chapters, we saw that political and labor leaders can set agendas for individual family members through citizen-ship requirements and certification processes. In this chapter we will focus on ways in which educators can set agendas for language minor-ity families through programs specifically designed to deal with family literacy practices. We will also examine how researchers in family literacy practices can set agendas by providing a theoretical orientation for family literacy programs.

In order to understand how family members can set literacy agendas for one another, we begin by discussing some of the research findings on the literacy practices of language minority families. We also discuss the findings, methods, and ideologies of such studies. Then we ex-amine the literacy agendas that educators set through family literacy programs and point out how many of the programs have been informed by the research on family literacy practices. We also discuss the goals of such programs with regard to preparing children for mainstream school experiences. Finally, we examine family literacy in the total context of language minority family life, noting how English literacy ranks in relation to other family needs and how it affects family dynamics. Before dealing with these issues, however, we turn to an overview of the role of literacy in the family.

The role of literacy in the family

The relationship between literacy and the family can be viewed in two ways. First, there is the role of literacy in the family; second, there is the role of family members in the development of literacy abilities. In examining the former, ethnographic researchers have studied how individual families use and talk about the printed material in their homes. They have spent time with families, documenting how the members interact around the printed word. Leichter (1984), for ex-ample, notes that in the many English-speaking families she inves-tigated, a great variety of visual forms was present in the home, ranging from books and maps to baseball cards and greeting cards. These various printed materials formed the basis for interactions which Heath (1980) calls *literacy events* (i.e., interactions based on the printed word), which occurred within a stream of everyday family activities. One of the principal purposes of Leichter's (1984) study was to document the exact role that literacy events played in the family.

Families also play a role in the development of literacy in that they foster certain uses of and attitudes toward literacy. In this way, families serve as literacy educators. The family's role in literacy education, however, may be quite different from that assumed by schools. As Leichter (1984) says:

While it may be argued that an educational curriculum or an educational agenda exists within families, . . . this curriculum is structured different-ly from that in schools in terms of both time and space, and it should be understood in its own terms. At best, formal instruction accounts for only a fraction of the education that takes place in families. Informal in-struction in the course of other activities – instruction that is often not even recognized as such – is essential for education within families, in-cluding the learning of literacy. (p. 38)

According to Leichter (1984, p. 38), families educate children not only in the use of the printed word but also in its value. They do this by evaluating children on how they use the printed word as well as by exhibiting (in the parents' own behavior) a certain attitude toward literacy.

What are the implications of such investigations for families such as the Trans and the Cierras? Some researchers argue that the manner in which families use language and value literacy is influenced to a great degree by external factors such as social class and cultural back-ground. Families such as the Trans and the Cierras, they argue, have culturally influenced ways of dealing with the printed word, ways that may be different from those typically displayed by mainstream fam-ilies. In light of these proposed differences, researchers often support one of two views toward the literacy uses of nonmainstream families: either that their literacy behavior is in some ways deficient or that it is simply different.

Those who attribute language minority children's difficulty in school to a lack of adequate literacy training in the home (Holtzman, Diaz-Guerrero, & Swartz, 1975; Jensen, 1973) are considered by some to be supporting a deficit model. On the other hand, those who uphold the worth of the way literacy is used and valued in the homes of language minority families (Delgado-Gaitan, 1987a, 1987b; Schief-felin & Cochran-Smith, 1984) are considered to be promoting a dif-ferent model. Proponents of both models, however, maintain that children from nonmainstream families will have a difficult time when they enter school because the uses of literacy that they have been exposed to in the home will not prepare them for the way language is used in mainstream classrooms. The influence of home literacy on school literacy and the desired goals of literacy education for non-

mainstream children are issues widely debated by educators. In order
to understand this, we turn first to a discussion of some of the studies
that have been undertaken regarding the relationship between language minority families and literacy, focusing on the use and value of
literacy in such families.

Research on language minority family literacy

Research on monolingual families

A seminal study on the relationship between literacy and the family
(one that has provided a model for much research on language minority family literacy) is that undertaken by Heath (1983). In studying the
communication patterns that existed in two communities in southern
United States – Roadville, a largely white community, and Trackton, a
largely black community – Heath argued that "the different ways children learned to use language were dependent on the ways in which each
community structured their families, defined the roles that community
members could assume, and played out their concepts of childhood
that guided child socialization" (p. 11). Heath maintains that in Roadville and Trackton, as in various communities throughout the world,
families and communities affect the ways in which children learn to
use language. In short, methods of communication vary because people's "communities have different social legacies and ways of behav-
ing in face-to-face interactions" (p. 11). The central question she
sought to answer was "what were the effects of the preschool home
and community environment on the learning of those language structures and uses which were needed in classrooms and job settings"
(p. 4).

In seeking an answer to this question, Heath (1983) employed an
ethnographic approach, describing in detail how children in their communities learned to use language and form values about how it func-
tioned in the community. She continued this approach in the classroom,
urging the town teachers to consider how language was used by students in their classes and encouraging them to use their insights about
classroom language "to move to new ways of *doing* in their classrooms" (p. 343). Heath's study provided a model for subsequent research on the ways in which language is used in other communities,
including some that were home to language minorities. We turn now to
a discussion of several such studies.

Research on bilingual families

Schieffelin and Cochran-Smith (1984), for example, used an ethnographic perspective to study what literacy meant in three different communities: a "group of educated, school-oriented parents and their preschool-aged children from a Philadelphia suburb, a family in a traditionally nonliterate society in Papua New Guinea, and a number of Chinese families who left Vietnam and recently settled in Philadelphia" (p. 4). Based on their research, they contend that the three social groups had very different kinds of literacy and placed different values on them. The children in the Philadelphia suburb, they maintain, were learning a "broad kind of literacy," referred to as *functional literacy,* which entailed using print in their everyday social transactions with peers and adults to acquire information, solve problems, and acquire knowledge.

Schieffelin and Cochran-Smith report that without exception the families in this community read stories to their children frequently and regularly, and the children were encouraged to look at books independently. Print materials were used by the parents to verify and extend the children's experiences, to legitimize information, and to help children deal with their emotions. Although both the children and adults participated actively in literacy events, the adults took on the roles of teachers-helpers, completing whatever parts of literacy events that the children asked them to complete or that the adults felt the children could not handle. Schieffelin and Cochran-Smith used such specifics to support the idea that these children's interest in print did not emerge "naturally" but rather emerged from a particular literacy orientation fostered by the family.

In the Sino-Vietnamese families, on the other hand, the families viewed the acquisition of English literacy as a priority, but "the home was not like a literate environment, even though these people were members of a literate culture. Books and a general interest in print did not organize activities of preschool-aged children" (Schieffelin & Cochran-Smith, 1984, p. 22). They conclude that, if a literate environment is one in which there are books and other forms of print in abundance, as well as writing materials, these homes would not be considered a literate environment. Although the parents were literate in Chinese, they did not read to their children in Chinese and made little progress in teaching them to read Chinese. Furthermore, unlike the suburban group, the parents in these families were often introduced to English literacy through their children. Children often acted as translators for their parents, reading and explaining announcements that covered a wide range of topics and that were issued by a number of different institutions. In light of these findings, Schieffelin and Cochran-Smith conclude that, in contrast to the uses of literacy in the suburban group, the uses of literacy in these families did not support the uses of literacy exhibited in many mainstream classrooms, in which the use of print is encouraged by the teacher to extend experiences, acquire information, and solve problems.

Although the methodology of the study, as we shall point out short-ly, has been criticized, such findings have nevertheless been used to bolster the idea that communities differ in their preschool literacy behavior and that some of these patterns are more congruent with those literacy behaviors valued by the mainstream educational setting. The approach adopted in the study is a typical one in which the literacy behavior of language minority families is contrasted with that of mainstream families, with the intention of documenting these differen-ces. By emphasizing the differences in the way families deal with print material, such studies, as we shall see, have led policymakers to pose the question of how best to deal with these differences in implement-ing literacy education programs.

Another ethnographic study that deals with family literacy in language minority communities is that undertaken by Delgado-Gaitan (1987a). Her focus was primarily on how the adults in the family used and valued literacy, both English and Spanish. Employing an ethnographic method-ology also, Delgado-Gaitan studied the literacy forms used among eight Mexican immigrant families in La Perla, California. The typical forms of literacy she found in these families' lives were family letters, religious books, storybooks, popular magazines, directions for household products, newspapers, school bulletins, and children's school texts. Of these forms, the most commonly read texts were letters from family members in Mexico and school bulletins.

Delgado-Gaitan found that for the adults in the family, reading had a functional value; it was used to perform household tasks and to assist the children in completing academic tasks. Rarely was it used for pleasure. Although the adults approached literacy in a functional man-ner, all held the acquisition of literacy, in both Spanish and English, in high esteem. All of the parents were anxious for their children to learn to read and write in English, viewing it as a key to their educational and economic success. Because of this belief, they rewarded children for their use of literacy in the home. For example, one parent in the study reported that she was so pleased when her two-year-old daughter would recite the alphabet when watching "Sesame Street," a children's television show, that she would hug her whenever she did so.

Based on her investigation, Delgado-Gaitan (1987a) draws four conclusions in regard to the value of literacy among the eight families:

(a) These families were grateful to be in the U.S. where conditions were relatively better than those in Mexico. They were aware of socio-political and economic limitations, but hoped that their situations would improve once they learned English. (b) Written text played an important role in these households. . . . (c) Motivation to learn English stemmed from many sources, from personal embarrassment at not knowing English to a desperate need to obtain steady employment. The adults in this study saw their position in society as oppressed but not necessarily hopeless, since they attributed most of their low socioeconomic condition to their inadequate English literacy skills. (d) Schooling was held in high regard by these families. Every adult in the study regarded schools as an important route to better education for their children and then to greater employment opportunities. Although parents did not speak English well, they assisted their children intellectually, in the way that they encouraged the children to study and explained the consequences of education. (pp. 28–29)

Whereas the Delgado-Gaitan (1987a) study attests to the value parents place on literacy development for their children, another study of Hispanic students argues that, although many language minority families may value literacy, the type of literacy behavior that occurs in Hispanic homes does not promote the high-level literacy skills they desire for their children. Employing an ethnographic methodology, Trueba (1984) investigated the way texts were used by twenty-seven lower-class Hispanic youths in their homes. Trueba (1984) distinguished eight literacy forms ranging from relatively easy forms (such as schedules and brief notes) to readings and writings of complicated materials and school-related tasks. He also distinguished three functions of literacy dealing with what he termed *literacy to do, literacy to know,* and *literacy to learn.* Finally, he posited a spectrum of values toward literacy ranging from −4 to +8. Youths who believed that reading and writing tasks were meaningless or difficult were rated as −4 while youths who believed that reading and writing were important for knowledge and economic survival were rated as +8.

Trueba's (1984) investigation of the way Hispanic youths used and valued texts in their homes resulted in the following findings. First, only three of the twenty-seven students expressed negative values toward literacy. For the rest of the youths, reading and writing were considered important for obtaining knowledge and jobs. In terms of the way print was used by the youths in their homes, thirteen of them engaged in reading for enjoyment, but only four of them did it regularly, and two of them concentrated on the Bible and religious reading. In fact, for some students their entire family would engage in reading the Bible and writing spiritual notes and messages in conjunction with the Bible. Trueba (1984) concludes that the "literacy context, motivation and specific functions of reading the Bible are in contrast with the enjoyment of reading activities which expose students to texts more like those found in textbooks and regular reading materials" (p. 32). Such a conclusion suggests that even though the students were involved with texts, the uses they made of these texts were atypical and thus did not prepare them for more mainstream uses of texts. It is a conclusion that goes beyond the findings of the study, emphasizing that the uses of literacy in these families differ from what are considered typical reading patterns.

Trueba also found that the students in their homes tended not to make much use of form E (reading of books for personal enjoyment) or form G (reading of long and complicated materials associated with work outside of school). In reporting this finding, Trueba (1984) notes that although the fieldworkers "did not expect to see much activity of the type classified as forms E and G, their feeling was that in Anglo-American families there is a greater frequency of such activities" (p. 32). Such a statement again reflects a belief that the kinds of texts read by Hispanic youths differ significantly from those read by mainstream youths, an assertion that is unsupported. Furthermore, it once again exemplifies a research perspective that emphasizes the uniqueness of language minority family behavior in comparison to mainstream families.

Trueba concludes that youths such as those in his study will never attain the literacy skills needed to succeed in school and in society at large. As he (1984) says:

The cornerstone of acculturation . . . is the capacity of newcomers to deal with English text. No other institution, no other activities have more direct and forceful influence than the school and the interaction with text. . . . The crucial role of the school is enhanced by the sociocultural isolation of many ethnolinguistic minority families, by their economic deprivation and their overall social background (so distant from middle class Anglo American children). The acquisition of literacy for Hispanic youth is at times a dream full of promises for the entire family, and at times, a painful and unwanted task needed for survival in school and in society. (p. 36)

According to Trueba (1984), one of the primary reasons that such youths will not succeed in school has to do with the role of the parents in their literacy development. As he puts it:

The role of parents whose literacy in English does not exist and who often do not have a functional level of literacy in Spanish is critical; by omission they may forfeit their right and obligation to support their children's education. They want to help but they do not know how. (p. 37)

Viewed from this perspective, the parents of language minority families appear to be the source of their children's educational problems. The argument seems to be that parents such as the Trans and the Cierras cannot provide their children with the necessary help to develop their literacy abilities. Because language minority children are unable to get this help at home, they are less likely to achieve high-level literacy abilities. Lacking these abilities, they will fail in school and ultimately fail in the larger socioeconomic context.

Studies on language minority families such as those already cited can set agendas for approaches to family literacy in that they are often used as the theoretical foundation for educational programs. Their findings, however, can be questioned on two grounds: their methodology and their ideology. Many of the studies on language minority families and literacy employ an ethnographic approach in order to document the uses of literacy found in language minority families and the role of these families as literacy educators. This current reliance on ethnographic methods to study family literacy is a practice that Stuckey (1991) questions. Stuckey (1991) maintains that the freshness of the ethnographic perspective "may excuse its incompleteness and sidestep an important issue: how ethnographic research presumes to contribute to an understanding of literacy. What, we may ask bluntly, do ethnographers of literacy want?" (p. 43). Referring specifically to the Schieffelin and Cochran-Smith (1984) study cited at the beginning of this chapter, Stuckey (1991) argues that for some ethnographers, "literacy events" are events in which literacy occurs, and literacy is a "litany of print" including such items as name labels, books, booklets, and magazines (p. 46). According to Stuckey (1991), the various printed media cited in some ethnographic studies are presented separate from content.

This tendency is evident in the study by Delgado-Gaitan (1987a), cited earlier, which listed the literacy forms used in the homes of the Mexican family members, without any indication as to their content or in general to the manner in which they were used in the home. Thus, the study lists such literacy forms as newspapers, school bulletins, letters from family members and prayer books as being used in the home but does not discuss how they were used or what they said. Because of this, the reader is left to wonder what the school bulletin said and how the family members reacted to the content.

Stuckey (1991) points out a similar problem of not giving attention to content in the study by Schieffelin and Cochran-Smith. In the study, Schieffelin and Cochran-Smith reprint a story written by a young Vietnamese student, emphasizing the fact that the story provides an example of how the child is able to use a narrative mode. The story is about a wise man who gives a child a magic book that the child cannot read. When the child tells the magic book he wishes he could read, his wish is granted and he can read. For Stuckey (1991, p. 50), the content, more than the form, provides insight into the refugee's relationship to literacy, a fact not brought out in the study. A potential shortcoming of ethnographic research, then – true of some ethnographic research but by no means all – is that in documenting the presence of print in the home, it may neglect to give attention to the content of what is being read and the reason it is being read. In addition to documenting that families are involved in reading such things as school bulletins, Stuckey would argue that describing the content of the bulletins and the reaction of families to the content will provide important insights beyond just the fact that families read. Whereas shortcomings such as these may be evident in some ethnographic research, it would be a mistake to discount all ethnographic research on this basis.

A second basis on which the findings of some ethnographic research may be challenged is their ideology. As in the studies already cited, some studies of family literacy focus on documenting the uniqueness of the way that literacy forms are used in language minority families. Frequently, the underlying assumption of such studies is that the way these families use literacy differs substantially from the way literacy is used in mainstream homes and classrooms. These differences, some argue, contribute to language minority children's relative lack of success in mainstream classrooms. The idea that home literacy is a primary cause of success (or lack of it) in school is in many cases considered to be a given. The suggestion that there may, in fact, be a great variety of social and economic factors (e.g., schools being poorly suited to meet the needs of language minority families) that lead to an individual's relative success (or lack of it) in the schools is rarely developed. In addition, the solution that is sometimes suggested is a purely linguistic one. Some argue that if children of language minority families are helped to develop their literacy skills, their success in school and the society at large will follow. Stuckey (1991, p. 41) questions this assumption by posing the question: "Why, we must ask, do studies of language always result in solutions that are linguistic rather than social or economic?" Although the methodology and ideology underlying some research on language minority family literacy may be questioned, their findings have been used, nonetheless, in some cases as a basis for the development of programs that address literacy in a family context. We turn now to a discussion of some of these programs.

Family literacy programs

Currently in the United States, there is a concern with the way families contribute to literacy development as evidenced in initiatives such as the Barbara Bush Family Literacy Foundation, Even Start legislation, and the Family English Literacy Program of the Office of Bilingual Education and Minority Languages Affairs (Auerbach, 1990, p. 14). This attention to family literacy is part of a national so-called literacy crisis, in which illiteracy is blamed for a variety of social problems such as homelessness, unemployment, and drug abuse. As a solution to the literacy problem, national policymakers have argued that the United States must look beyond the school system to the family in order to understand the literacy crisis. As former Secretary of Education Terrel Bell puts it, "Not even the best classroom can make up for failure in the family" (as cited in Auerbach, 1990, p. 14). A prevalent idea in the rhetoric surrounding the literacy crisis is that a lack of support for literacy in families leads to illiteracy among children, which then continues a vicious cycle. The way to break this cycle is to address issues of literacy in the family. Some even compare the situation to a hereditary illness. As one columnist in a major newspaper puts it:

The point is that literacy, like illiteracy, is a heritable trait; children catch it from their parents. And it may be that the best way to launch an attack on illiteracy is to treat it as a family disease. (W. Raspberry, "Barbara Bush's Pet Project," *Washington Post,* March 11, 1989, as cited in Auerbach, 1990, p. 14)

It is in the context of such discussions that U.S. family literacy programs for language minorities have developed. For some, the primary purpose of these programs is to help language minority parents support the school achievement of their children. As Weinstein-Shr (1990, pp. 1–2) points out, those who support this goal believe it can be attained through a variety of measures. One measure is to encourage parents to monitor their children's school work, tutor them, and communicate with school personnel. Another way is to demonstrate for language minority parents the early reading strategies (such as reading aloud) that exist in the homes of successful readers. When parents are not literate in English, this model is reversed so that language minority children are encouraged to read to their parents. Finally, some programs seek to support parents' involvement in their children's academic success by including in the curriculum content and social issues that are relevant to the families.

Whereas language minority family literacy programs were originally designed as early intervention programs for young children, some programs now include literacy goals for adults. These goals include the following:

1) to provide parents with childrearing information and resources in a new culture; 2) to enhance parents' self-confidence and self-esteem, which, in turn, will contribute to their children's literacy development; 3) to empower parents to connect literacy activities to their own social and cultural situations; and 4) to provide literacy skills that may lead to other education and workplace skills. (Rangel, 1990, p. 6)

In contrast to these goals, some family literacy programs include practices that focus exclusively on teaching parents how to promote their children's success in school, including practices such as the following:

Teaching parents about the American educational system and philosophy of schooling

Providing parents with concrete methods and materials to use at home with children

Assisting parents to promote "good reading habits"

Training parents for home tutoring in basic skills . . .

Giving parents guidelines and techniques for helping with homework

Training parents in how to read to children or listen to children read

Training in "effective parenting"

Teaching parents to make and play games to reinforce skills

Teaching parents how to communicate with school authorities

(Auerbach, 1989, pp. 168–169)

Auerbach (1989) contends that family literacy programs that employ such practices exemplify what she terms a *transmission of school practices* model. Although the programs included under this model take various forms, they share a common agenda, namely, "to strengthen the ties between the home and the school by transmitting the culture of school literacy through the vehicle of the family" (p. 169).

Auerbach (1989) argues that the transmission model is a new version of a deficit model. In addition, she contends that it contains several assumptions that do not correspond to the realities of the lives of language minorities. The first assumption is that language minority students come from literacy-impoverished homes in which education is not valued or supported. In disputing this assumption, Auerbach points to the Delgado-Gaitan (1987a) study discussed earlier and the Harvard Families and Literacy Study (Chall & Snow, 1982) which found a range of literacy practices and materials in language minority homes.

Second, the transmission model assumes that family literacy involves a one-way transfer of skills *from* parent *to* children. However, literacy work with language minority families in the University of Massachusetts English Family Literacy Project showed that literacy practices in families is complex and not always unidirectional. Rather, family members each contribute in the areas where they are strongest, with the children often helping their parents with homework and acting as interpreters for them.

Third, the transmission model assumes that success in school is determined by parents' ability to support school-like activities in the home. In disputing this assumption, Auerbach cites the study by Chall and Snow (1982), which found that literacy development was affected by a variety of home factors, including the emotional climate of the home, the amount of time children spent interacting with adults, the level of financial stress, and the level of parental involvement with the schools.

The fourth assumption that Auerbach disputes is the idea that school practices are adequate and that it is home factors that determine who succeeds. She argues instead that both school factors and parental factors are important for literacy success. Finally, she disputes the assumption that parents' problems get in the way of literacy development and that they must be addressed outside the classroom as a precondition for progress. Instead, she maintains that such problems need to be acknowledged and explored in the classroom. In light of the shortcomings of the transmission model, Auerbach (1989) argues for a participatory family literacy program in which the goal

is to increase the social significance of literacy in family life by incorporating community cultural forms and social issues into the content of literacy activities. This model is built on the particular conditions, concerns, and cultural expertise of specific communities, and, as such, does not involve a predetermined curriculum or set of practices or activities. Instead, the curriculum development process is participatory and is based on a collaborative investigation of critical issues in family or community life. (p. 177)

Although the participatory model supported by Auerbach does not support the assimilationist perspective of the transmission model, it nonetheless has its own agenda. The agenda is to involve parents and community leaders in the curriculum design of family literacy programs. In some cases, however, language minority parents, because of their own culturally influenced view of education, may be reluctant to become involved in educational decisions. Studies of Vietnamese parents, for example, point out that although Vietnamese parents strongly support education, believing that it will determine their children's future, they are reluctant to participate in school matters because they feel that educational matters should be left to teachers and administrators. In addition, some parents are reluctant to participate because of their lack of English skills, whereas others are unable to do so because of the effort they must expend on their economic survival (California State Department of Education, 1982, p. 5).

Studies such as these suggest that there may be various reasons why parents like the Cierras and the Trans may be unable or unwilling to participate in the design of family literacy programs. Family literacy programs, then, even when they encourage community and parent participation, set agendas for literacy development, agendas that language minority parents themselves may be unwilling or unable to accept. However, regardless of the approach taken by family literacy programs, all such programs share the goal of developing the participants' literacy abilities. The question is, then, what kind of literacy needs to be developed? If, as ethnographic studies suggest, immigrant families exemplify literacy practices that differ from mainstream literacy practices, do language minority children need to learn mainstream ways of using words in order to succeed in school? If so, once they acquire this mainstream literacy, will they be successful in school and ultimately in the larger social context? These are the questions we turn to now.

Family literacy and school literacy

Several studies have documented the fact that the children of language minority families such as the Trans and the Cierras frequently have lower academic achievement than do children from mainstream homes (Sue & Padilla, 1986; Trueba, 1989). In explaining this fact, some linguists and educators, as we have pointed out, contend that language differences are a primary reason for language minority children's lack of success in school. At the same time, they reject the notion that the way language and literacy are used in language minority families is in any way deficient. Rather, they maintain that the reason language minority children do not succeed in schools is that there is a mismatch between home literacy practices and school literacy practices. Underlying this perspective is the assumption that the skills and literacy abilities learned in one community may be more or less productive in another. When the skills and literacy abilities learned in the home environment are not productive in the school environment, language minority children need to learn the ways of using words that are valued by mainstream institutions such as public schools. Schools, too, may have to strive to "improve the fit of the two cultures in contact" (Sue & Padilla, 1986, pp. 47–48).

One proponent of this approach is Heath (1986), who contends that many language minority children, particularly those in low or threatened socioeconomic positions (such as the Trans and the Cierras), "neither seek extensive interactions with outside or mainstream institutions nor create and manage analogous institutions within their own communities. Hence, the children from these groups often come to school bringing language uses and cultural beliefs supporting ways of using language that differ greatly from those of the classroom" (p. 147). On the other hand, schools often expect not only that, when children enter school, they will be able to speak English but also that "they have internalized *before* they start to school the norms of language used in academic life" (p. 148). These uses involve such activities as using language to label and describe things, to recount or recast past events, to follow directions, to maintain social interactions, and to obtain information. There is, then, a mismatch between the literacy practices that language minority children learn before school and those that the school expects of children when they enter school.

Heath (1986) maintains that in order for language minority children to succeed in school, they "must have – in either their mother tongue or English – multiple, repeated, and reinforced access to certain language uses that match those of the school" (p. 174). When language minority children do not have such language uses available, it is the responsibility of the school to promote these uses of language. As Heath (1986) puts it:

Must the school bear the major burden for preparing language-minority children for the kinds of performances in English that the world of work requires? Yes. Though it is possible that other mainstream institutions such as the church, labor union, voluntary associations, and the public media may play some role in modeling and giving practice for the genres noted here, communities tolerate the instructions of these secondary institutions only to a certain extent. (p. 181)

In addition, Heath is skeptical that early intervention programs such as the family literacy programs discussed earlier will be able to accomplish the task. As she says:

Most language-minority communities are reluctant to accept parent education from outsiders; rearing children is a private or community responsibility, and rare is the group that freely allows strangers to tell them how to socialize their young to language or anything else. Thus, parent education programs that set out to teach parents how to raise their children so they will be linguistically prepared for school have relatively little chance of achieving far- reaching influence. The desire for change in such a core value as how one socializes the young must come from within a group; trying to impose external values on preschool home life is not likely to bring any significant internal change to families. (p. 181)

In rejecting the likely success of family literacy programs, Heath places the burden for teaching minority children mainstream literacy practices on the schools. The agenda nonetheless seems to be that language minority children need to acquire mainstream uses of language in order to succeed in school and ultimately in the larger society.

For Stuckey (1991), one of the central questions involved in reconciling the plurality of community literacies with the mainstream literacy promoted in school settings is the issue of whether language minority children should acquire those literacies that are valued by the dominant society in school. If so, will this resolve the social inequality that exists in the society? Stuckey explores this issue by questioning whether language minority children will gain more power in society if they acquire mainstream ways of using language. Stuckey (1991) contends that Heath, by answering this question in the affirmative, lends support to the notion that "if we teach students to communicate in mainstream ways, then society will become more equal and just" (Stuckey, 1991, p. 39). Stuckey refuses to accept this conclusion, pointing out that as Heath herself notes in reference to the language uses of blacks and whites in southern United States, the actual language habits of Southern whites and blacks are close. Thus, it is not different language uses that are the cause of social, economic, and educational differences between whites and blacks. Rather, Stuckey argues, the differences between the groups reside in larger social and economic issues, involving the way in which the political and economic structure itself provides or fails to provide for equal opportunity. For Stuckey (1991, p. 41), the question of inequality among social groups warrants not just linguistic solutions but also social and economic answers.

In challenging the role that literacy programs can play in addressing social inequality, Stuckey suggests a need for educators to examine the larger social and economic issues that affect the lives of language minorities. Whereas many of the studies cited earlier focused exclusively on literacy practices in language minority families, other studies have looked at literacy issues in a broader context. Some of them have examined how literacy issues are valued by language minorities in reference to other problems they face. Others have explored the effect of acquiring English literacy on the dynamics of language minority families. We turn now to an examination of several such studies.

Family literacy in context

How does the acquisition of second language literacy rank in the priority of needs of language minority families? Most discussions of second language literacy argue that language minority families place the acquisition of English high on their priority list as a means of bettering their social and economic condition. Delgado-Gaitan (1987a, p. 19), for example, maintains that the Mexican families she worked with appeared to be interested "in improving their social and economic conditions through acquiring higher literacy skills." Schieffelin and Cochran-Smith (1984, p. 21) also note that "for the recently arrived refugees, the acquisition of functional literacy in English is a priority." The question is how this desire ranks in relation to their other needs.

Some insight into this issue is provided in a study by Hogeland and Rosen (1990) on undocumented women in the United States. Part of this study involved interviewing 413 undocumented women, asking them to rank the services that they felt were especially important for their families. The list included twenty-seven different services (including such things as child care, marriage counseling, alcohol programs, and English literacy programs), of which they were to select five. One fact that the study illustrated was that different communities ranked these services in different ways. The 56 Filipina women, for example, rated the services in the following order: medical services, most important, followed by employment placement, immigration assistance, housing, and health insurance (p. 51). The 345 Latina women, on the other hand, ranked them as follows: housing as most important, followed by employment training, medical services, employment placement, immigration assistance, child care, and finally, English programs (p. 67).

The difference in these priorities illustrates how different communities and different families have different needs. Because all of those interviewed were undocumented women, all of them placed immigration assistance high on the list. On the other hand, the Filipina women in general did not see language training as one of the most important services, perhaps due to their own familiarity with spoken English. For the Latina women, on the other hand, housing and employment issues, medical care, and child care were all more important than was language training. Such rankings provide insight into agendas of the language minority families themselves; even more insightful are the comments the immigrant women made in regard to the effect of immigration on their families.

Several Filipina women, for example, pointed to the stress they felt in leaving their children back in the Philippines. Some were concerned about the relationship they had with their children. As one woman put it, "I am having trouble with my son. He likes the fast pace, technical environment here. He does not listen to me as he should" (p. 47). One official of the Filipino community points out that "every dining room table in the Filipino family is a battlefield between the old and young. Old people would like to see old traditions and customs kept, even in this new environment. But for the young, integration is inevitable" (Father Antonio Rey, as cited in Hogeland & Rosen, 1990, p. 29). Other women described the physical violence that occurred in the family owing to pressures of unemployment and crowded living conditions. Some women stated that the pressure of immigration had affected their marriage so that they were left with children and no jobs. Some Latina women pointed out that, although they came to the

United States without their children so that they could "make a better life" for their children, they were disappointed that they were not able to make enough money to send anything back. Another concern was the problem of dependency on family members for survival. As one woman put it, "I live with my niece and her husband. He is constantly harassing her and told her if she has another baby, he will not be able to support the family. I am fearful because I don't have anywhere else to go" (Hogeland & Rosen, 1990, p. 60).

Even when family members want to improve their literacy abilities, various economic and social factors, such as we have examined in previous chapters, will undermine their ability to accomplish this goal. Hogeland and Rosen (1990, p. 28), for example, point out that one study of immigrant women found that, although women had a strong desire to learn English, they were not able to attend classes because of their work schedules and the responsibility of running their homes. Employers, too, discouraged their workers from learning English out of fear that if the workers did so, they might increase their earning power and their ability to organize through labor unions.

Studies such as this suggest that immigrant families face a host of problems ranging from family violence to intergenerational misunderstandings to economic stress. Resolving these issues is undoubtedly high on their personal and family agendas. Where literacy ranks in this list is a difficult question. Although immigrants such as the Trans and the Cierras may have a desire for their families to become literate in English, what they see as more pressing agendas (such as jobs, medical care, and adequate housing) may well take precedence over the agendas of English literacy. The conflicts that exist among these agendas may mean that second language literacy agendas, even if they are considered essential or desirable, will have to be put aside. As we shall see in the next chapter, one literacy curriculum possibility is to use such conflicts as the basis for reflection and possible action.

Another study that views English literacy in the total family context is that completed by Wong Fillmore (1991), who sought to determine the effects of the acquisition of English literacy on the dynamics of the family. Wong Fillmore undertook a nationwide survey of language shift among language minority children in the United States. Eleven hundred families were surveyed to determine the extent to which the children's early learning of English in preschools affected family language patterns. Three hundred eleven families whose children attended a preschool program conducted exclusively in Spanish served as the control group for a comparison with families in the main sample group whose children attended English-only or bilingual preschools. Not surprisingly, the children in the main sample reported using the home language less frequently and English more frequently than did the children in the control group. What is important, however, is the effect of this shift on family dynamics.

Many parents in the main sample reported that, although English was not a language they were able to use easily to express themselves, they nevertheless were using it in speaking to their children. In contrast with the control group, in which almost 94 percent reported using their own language exclusively or mostly with their children, only 78 percent of the main sample did so (p. 337). In light of these findings, Wong Fillmore (1991) asks what happens to family relations when the language children give up is the language the parents speak. For Wong Fillmore (1991):

What is lost is no less than the means by which parents socialize their children – when parents are unable to talk to their children, they cannot easily convey to them their values, beliefs, understandings or wisdom about how to cope with their experiences. They can not teach them about the meaning of work, or about personal responsibility, or what it means to be a moral or ethical person in a world with too many choices and too few guideposts to follow. (p. 343)

Beyond this inability, the children's lack of familiarity with their parents' language can result in misunderstandings and even violence. Wong Fillmore, for example, relates the case of one of the families in the study in which Korean children's unfamiliarity with the honorifics of Korean led them to offend their grandfather, who had recently come to visit them from overseas. The grandfather, offended by such disrespect, conveyed this to his son, who in turn did what was required of him. He beat the children for their disrespect and rudeness. Studies such as this document how, as language minority children shift to a use of English, both parents and children may suffer greatly.

As roles in the family shift, both parents and children may be under stress. As Hogeland and Rosen (1990) point out:

Immigrant children become "Americanized" much faster than their parents, due in large part to their contact with the educational system. Due to their rapid acculturation process, they are forced into the role of helping the parents navigate their way through the "system." This creates stress for the child, who feels overburdened by the responsibility, and for the parents, who feel they are losing their parental authority. (pp. 28–29)

Díaz, Moll, and Mehan (1986, p. 210) note a similar problem, pointing out that when language minority children, because of their English proficiency, take responsibility for contacts with social institutions, they assume power and control usually reserved for the adults in the family.

In light of the possible negative consequences of the acquisition of English literacy on language minority families, Weinstein-Shr (in press) argues that educational agendas for language minority literacy should not be limited to promoting the children's school achievement, but should be based on extensive research of the literacy needs of the families. Such research would explore three sets of questions:

1. How do refugees, immigrants (or any families served by schools) solve or fail to solve problems that require literacy skills? . . .
2. What are the functions and uses of literacy (both native and second language) in the lives of people that are served? Who uses what language and to whom and under what circumstances? What are the consequences of this particular communicative economy? What are the implications for home-school communications (including the parents' experience of those communications)?
3. What is the significance of language in the negotiation of new roles and relationships in a new setting? How has authority and power shifted in families? What is the role of language in intergenerational relationships? What are the ways in which schools influence the process in which these relationships are negotiated?

The findings of such research would provide insight into how language minorities themselves value the development of English literacy relative to other goals they have. Furthermore, the research would demonstrate how the acquisition of English literacy can affect the relationships of family members. Such information is critical to the development of educational programs if the programs are to respond in any way to the literacy agendas of language minority families themselves.

Summary and implications

In this chapter we have examined various agendas that affect the development of English literacy among language minority families. We have reviewed the findings of studies on English literacy practices in language minority families, noting how such studies demonstrate the way in which literacy agendas are set within a family by family members interacting with one another. Language minority parents, for example, anxious for their children to acquire English literacy, can set literacy agendas for their children in order to help them develop their ability to deal with English texts. When language minority parents are not literate in English, they can set literacy agendas for their children by asking them to translate written texts in English for them. Children, on the other hand, can set literacy agendas for their parents by bringing home literacy tasks from their school environment. In addition, we have explored the methodology and ideology of these studies and demonstrated how their findings have provided the basis for the design of some family literacy programs.

This chapter has also discussed how family literacy programs can set literacy agendas. We have examined the overall goals of such programs, questioning whether the acquisition of mainstream literacy practices by language minority children will reduce social inequalities. Finally, we have discussed the acquisition of English literacy in the total context of language minority families. By reviewing studies on language minority families, we have seen that English literacy, although an important agenda in the lives of language minority families, may be overshadowed by other social and economic agendas. Furthermore, the acquisition of English literacy among some members of the family, particularly when involving a loss of the mother tongue, can have serious consequences on the overall dynamics of family life.

What are the implications of this discussion for second language literacy researchers and educators? Observing how language minority families interact around a written text, both in English and the mother tongue, can provide valuable information for understanding the literacy needs and agendas of language minority families. The danger, however, is that in reporting such observations, researchers may compare the literacy practices of language minority families with mainstream families. In doing so they may suggest that, because the literacy practices of minority families are in some instances different from those of mainstream families, they are inadequate. Such a suggestion may be used to promote a deficit model of language minority families. Furthermore, documenting differences in literacy practices can result in such language differences being viewed as the primary cause of children's success (or lack of success) in mainstream classrooms, thus minimizing the fact that many factors – both in the school and in the larger social structure – can affect school achievement. These are dangers that need to be considered in both undertaking and evaluating family literacy research.

Second language literacy educators need to thoroughly examine the goals of family literacy programs. Is their primary purpose to help language minority children succeed in mainstream classrooms? If so, does this mean that language minority families need to acquire mainstream patterns of parenting and using literacy so that the children can achieve academic success, resulting in a program that adheres to the transmission of school practices model? If this is not the primary goal of such programs, what are their goals? Should they derive from educators, from language minority family members, or from both? If the goals should be derived solely or in part from language minority family members, how can educators determine these goals if language minorities are hesitant to participate in educational decision making? These are difficult questions that need to be addressed in the design of family literacy programs.

Finally, second language literacy educators need to recognize that, whereas developing English literacy abilities can be important to language minority families, there may be other family agendas that are far more pressing, many of which arise from living in a new culture in which traditional family values may be challenged. Indeed, the development of English literacy itself may be seen as a threat to family values and parental authority. In order to minimize the negative effect that the development of English literacy can have on the dynamics of the family, it is essential for family literacy programs to strive to develop mother tongue literacy. Clearly, the reasons for doing so are many. Using parents to teach mother tongue literacy can be rewarding for the parents and the children. Placing value on mother tongue literacy may also help children in their academic success. Most important, promoting mother tongue literacy not only develops an important language resource but also may have positive effects on reducing intergenerational conflicts.

Family literacy programs are only one of several types of educational programs designed to meet the literacy agendas of language minorities. In the next chapter we will examine other types of second language literacy programs and focus on how they might be evaluated. We will also discuss various orientations to second language literacy curricula and the factors that affect the design and selection of these curricula. Finally, we will explore the rationale for second language assessment as well as measures for such assessment on both a national and program level.

5 Educational agendas for second language literacy

Because or her shyness and fear, Hoa Tran has never attended a literacy class. Minh Tran, on the other hand, in hopes of gaining the literacy skills necessary to get certified to work as a medical technologist, has enrolled in several classes. Carlos Cierra, too, has attended several English classes, one of which was designed to qualify him for an amnesty program. His wife, Maria, has also attended classes, but whenever she is able to get a job cleaning houses or offices, she doesn't attend. Sometimes problems with finding someone to take care of the children prevent her from attending classes. Melchora Galang has signed up for several literacy classes, but her various jobs and long work schedule have often made it difficult for her to continue the classes.

The agendas of various literacy interest groups can influence the kinds of literacy programs that are available to people such as the Trans, the Cierras, and the Galangs. Funders, for example, who want some assurance that their money is well spent, can require certain types of literacy assessment in a program. Curriculum designers, holding certain values regarding what should be taught in a literacy class, can set class content agendas through the types of curricula they design. Teachers, faced with certain administrative demands and beliefs about their roles, can set agendas in enacting a curriculum and assessing literacy. In contrast, learners have their own educational agendas and have certain literacy goals they wish to attain and practical limitations to attaining those goals. The manner in which their agendas may conflict with the agendas of funders, curriculum designers, and teachers is one focus of this chapter.

In this chapter we will examine the manner in which educational agendas for second language literacy are set by three factors of the educational environment: program design, curriculum design, and assessment strategies. To begin, we will distinguish various types of literacy programs and examine the agendas that can affect the design of literacy programs. Next, we will describe several literacy programs, illustrating the various dimensions by which programs can differ.

Finally, we will consider the basis on which such programs might be evaluated. In the area of curriculum design, we will explore the agendas that can affect the design and selection of stated curricula. We will also consider who can set the agenda in the implementation of a curriculum. Finally, we will consider who can set assessment agendas, what measures can be used to assess learners' progress, and why assessment is undertaken. Before dealing with these issues, however, we will discuss the role of literacy in education.

The role of literacy in education

Literacy in an educational context can be viewed in one of two ways: as the product of education or as the basis for it. When it is viewed from the former perspective, literacy is seen as a set of skills related to the printed word that develop from educational training. In the area of reading, Haverson (1991) terms this perspective a *skills-based approach* (p. 185). In such an approach, "great emphasis is placed on the mastery of sound-symbol relationships" based on the underlying assumption that, once an individual masters this skill, meaning will follow. A variation of this model identifies four areas of language: vocabulary, sound-symbol relationships, grammar, and comprehension. Each area is taught separately in the belief that meaning will follow if these skills are integrated by the reader (Haverson, 1991, p. 186).

Critics such as Langer (1987), however, argue that this kind of literacy education exemplifies a kind of education that is curriculum driven in which

there is a set of skills or information to be learned, and the teacher tests to see what the students know or don't know, teaches what isn't known, then tests to see if it has been learned. Perhaps more by accident than by design, when instruction is driven by this mode, the focus shifts almost inevitably toward discrete skills and items of information that are easy to test, and away from deeper understandings that are more complicated and time-consuming to consider. (p. 10)

Those who criticize a product- or skill-based view of literacy prefer to view literacy as a process- or strategy-based endeavor. According to Langer (1987), from this perspective literacy is the ability to think and reason. It is a tool that enables "a thinking about language and about oral and written discourse, using language to extend meanings and knowledge about ideas and experiences" (p. 2). Literacy education, then, is not the product of training in specific skills, but a process by which people learn how to do new things "in contexts where the learner is engaged with others in carrying out socially meaningful tasks" (Langer, 1987, p. 11). Literacy is not taught as a set of discrete skills; it develops "when learners see models of literate behavior as other people engage in literacy activities, and when they talk and ask questions about what is happening, why and how" (Langer, 1987, p. 11). Reading, from this perspective, involves the "successful inter- action of conceptual abilities, background knowledge, and processing strategies (Haverson, 1991, p. 186).

As shall be pointed out later in the chapter, frequently literacy curricula and assessment measures reflect one view or the other of literacy. In tending to employ either a skill-based or process-based perspective in their work, curriculum and test designers set second language literacy agendas. Before considering this issue, however, we turn to a discussion of the design of various literacy programs, pointing out the dimensions by which they can vary. We also examine by what standards such programs might be judged and consider how program evaluation can affect the implementation of literacy programs.

Second language literacy programs

Types of programs

In analyzing adult literacy education in the United States, Fingeret (1984) distinguishes two types of programs: individually oriented pro- grams, which serve the individual in isolation from the community, and community-oriented programs, which are designed to aid the individual in a community context. "Individually oriented programs tend to approach literacy as the primary focus of instruction and to be oriented to 'mainstreaming' the individual into middle-class society" (p. 19). Although they may include content that deals with housing or employment, their primary goal is to teach literacy skills to increase an individual's economic self-sufficiency. Community-oriented programs, on the other hand, are more likely to be advocates of social change. What is considered to be functional literacy is defined by the com- munity's reality; "reading is secondary to developing an understanding of social forces and a belief in cooperative effort and the possibility of change" (p. 21). Fingeret contends that individually oriented programs predominate in the United States. Most federally sponsored programs are based on "the assumption that literacy is a set of skills, that illiteracy is a cause of many of the problems encountered by poor or minority persons, and that individual intervention, in the form of literacy instruction, can change an individual's socioeconomic and cultural status" (pp. 17–18).

In analyzing the Canadian context, Read and Mackay (1984) distinguish literacy programs that take place in institutionalized school settings from those that focus on the needs of learners in their communities. They contend that, although many literacy training courses exist throughout Canada, most of these programs take place in institutionalized school settings, with fixed-scheduled classes and tuition fees. On the other hand, there are alternative programs that are more flexible and less expensive that allow learners such as Maria and Melchora to attend classes. Read and Mackay (1984) examine a variety of such programs, describing them not "as prototypes to be duplicated" but "as examples of types of programs that have grown up in response to needs felt in their communities" (p. 110). In this sense, the programs reflect what Fingeret calls community-oriented programs. In order to illustrate the various dimensions by which second language literacy programs can differ and on what basis they might be evaluated, we will examine several of the Canadian second language literacy programs described by Read and Mackay.

Examples of programs

HELP A FRIEND LEARN ENGLISH

Help a Friend Learn English is a Toronto program that was developed by the Ministry of Citizenship and Culture primarily to meet the needs of elderly, shut-in Spanish-speaking language minorities. These language minorities are paired with a volunteer and use the telephone as the medium of instruction to conduct weekly English lessons. The volunteers, usually also elderly, use a bilingual text that is based on situations that center on the needs of language minorities. The program assumes some language literacy on the part of the learner. Read and Mackay (1984) point out that as the program exists it is very cheap to operate and requires minimal administrative expenses. However, local telephone rate increases may affect the willingness of volunteers to participate, a fact that illustrates how even external considerations such as phone rates can affect the successful implementation of a program. According to Read and Mackay (1984), evaluation of the program "confirmed that the main gain of its participants was friendship and confidence" (p. 112).

ACTION FOR LITERACY

The York program Action for Literacy, funded by a combination of provincial and federal money and employing fifty qualified teachers, was initiated to address the literacy needs of homebound learners. The program includes an intensive training period for the teachers, an ongoing professional development component, and extensive contact with community services and ethnic organizations. The content of each learner's course is based on his or her stated interests and needs. In order to accomplish this task, the teachers have access to a bank of suitable materials that they can use to meet the needs of their students on an ongoing basis. Learners in the program participate for a variety of reasons. Some have physical disabilities; others have day-care and work schedule problems; still others have negative feelings toward school or need help coping with other courses they are taking.

VIETNAMESE REFUGEES PROGRAM

The bilingual classes in the Alberta program for Vietnamese refugees use an English-speaking teacher and a Chinese/Vietnamese interpreter. During the initial three weeks, students receive basic information on Canada and its customs as well as information on local services through an interpreter. After an initial bilingual period, English instruction is begun. One of the major benefits of the program is that the initial training in the mother tongue helps to relieve the participants' major doubts and questions about life in Canada. According to Read and Mackay (1984, p. 121), the removal of this major stress factor allows participants to concentrate on learning English, knowing where to go for help should they need it. The program, however, is held only when there is a sufficient number of language minorities of the same linguistic background and literacy level to warrant a class, illustrating how feasibility issues can affect the availability of literacy programs.

FOCUS ON CHANGE

Focus on Change is a YMCA program designed for sole-support mothers who need to upgrade their skill in math and English in order to prepare for a job search. The program is free, with child care and bus tickets provided. According to the director, the purpose of the course is to help the participants develop their communication skills and some critical consciousness. In order to accomplish this task, women discuss issues relevant to women's lives, for example, information on self-defense techniques for women. According to Read and Mackay (1984), the program "attempts to contextualize literacy: helping powerless people to express their opinions in constructive ways. The approach recognizes the participants as reasoning beings able to analyze their lives and attempt to solve their own problems" (p. 123).

Program evaluation

Given such a wide range of second language literacy programs, on what basis can they be evaluated? In discussing literacy program evaluation, Lytle and Wolfe (1989) point out that "because there is a lack of consensus about the purposes of literacy education, and because the field is by definition pluralistic, there can be no single definition of evaluation or assessment nor one view of what makes the best program" (p. 59). Generally, a determination of what constitutes a good literacy program depends on who is doing the evaluation. For example, in reference to the four programs just described, Read and Mackay (1984) list several criteria by which they evaluate the programs. In order to illustrate the various dimensions by which programs can be evaluated, we will consider their criteria and apply them to the four programs. The following are the characteristics Read and Mackay consider as important to successful second language literacy programs:

1. The teachers are qualified.
2. The program is intensive.
3. There are prepared materials.
4. The program is flexible in that the learners have a say in the design of the program.
5. There is a bilingual staff member available.
6. The program is community oriented in that it is based on the needs of the community it serves.
7. The program has an informal atmosphere.
8. The program has day-care facilities.
9. The course and materials are free.
10. The program teaches work skills.
11. The program includes orientation information regarding the community and culture.

12. The program builds the confidence of the learner.
13. The program is in a convenient location.

(Adapted from Read & Mackay, 1984, p. 118)

Employing these criteria, Read and Mackay (1984) rate Help a Friend Learn English as strong in having prepared materials, a bilingual component, an informal atmosphere, free materials, orientation information, confidence building and a convenient location. On the other hand, it is rated negatively in the sense that the teachers are not trained, it is not intensive, and there is no flexibility in the curriculum, no community orientation, and no day-care or work skills. In contrast to Help a Friend Learn English, Action for Literacy is rated positively on the basis of its qualified teachers, its flexibility in course materials, its attention to work skills, and its community orientation. Read and Mackay rate the program for Vietnamese refugees as strong in all areas except having prepared materials and work skills. Focus on Change is also rated positively on all aspects except having prepared materials and a bilingual component.

The standards set forth by Read and Mackay (1984) are not the only criteria that can be used to evaluate programs. Wrigley (1991), for example, delineates others in her evaluation of literacy programs in the United States. As part of a national research study funded by the U.S. Department of Education, Wrigley (1991) identified and studied effective and innovative second language literacy programs in the United States. Based on her observation of effective programs, she designed a profile of characteristics that educationally sound programs share, many of which reflect the assumptions of current literature on literacy education. In studying nine programs that matched the profile, the following findings emerged:

1. There was shared control and collaboration among the funders, staff, and learners even though the type of collaboration differed from site to site. In general, the programs included strong participation in selecting classroom content but weak participation in program design. In fact, very few programs had a formal mechanism that involved learners in decisions about overall program design. This finding suggests that program design, in contrast to curriculum design, is left largely to forces other than the participants themselves.
2. There was a learner-centered curriculum. Learners in the programs were involved in setting course goals, and the curriculum was flexible enough to allow for changes in response to their goals. In addition, even when there was a heterogeneous class, the curriculum tried to incorporate the students' experience and concerns into the course.

3. There was a balance between experiential literacy, which stresses the creative and problem-solving aspects of learning, and language awareness, in which there is a focus on traditional skills. Thus, both views of literacy described earlier in the chapter were included.
4. There was a method for assessing learner progress and documenting program effectiveness. Often administrators were more concerned with issues of outcomes and accountability than were teachers and learners, who seemed secure that they were being successful in developing literacy.

Standards by which programs are evaluated by researchers, then, differ depending on the views of the evaluators. Wrigley's standards place more emphasis on learner input in both program and curriculum design than do the standards set forth by Read and Mackay (1984). In both cases, however, the standards reflect to some extent the biases of the evaluators. The important question is: Who specifies such criteria and who determines whether they are positive or negative? Read and Mackay (1984) and Wrigley (1991) have set forth a list that includes many of the characteristics that researchers and educators today, given the paradigm under which they operate, consider to be positive elements of a literacy program, such as attention to community needs, materials that respond to student needs, and confidence building. They have, in other words, employed a set of criteria that literacy researchers and educators currently consider to be important. In so doing, to the extent they are involved in the implementation of literacy programs, they will set agendas for the design and evaluation of such programs. The implementation of literacy programs, however, does not involve the academic community alone. Program funders also are central to the design and implementation of literacy programs. How might this group evaluate the programs described?

From a funder's perspective, Help a Friend Learn English is an inexpensive program to operate and thus, in terms of cost efficiency, may be rated highly. Having trained teachers, a materials bank, and a professional development component are expensive undertakings. Hence, the very components that educators may rate positively, funders may see as negative in the sense that they increase costs. In the same way, the bilingual component of the Vietnamese refugee program and the day care at Focus for Change, although rated by Read and Mackay (1984) as a positive factor, may from a funder's perspective be seen as additional cost factors. The cost factor, of course, is not the only factor that funders consider. In some cases, particularly if the program is government funded, funders may need to justify the value of a program in terms of its ability to meet national literacy agendas. Literacy programs that focus on skill development for employability are generally more likely to get government support. As was pointed out in Chapter 3, most government-sponsored language and literacy programs in Canada have a work component. In the United States, as was mentioned earlier, federally funded literacy programs tend to emphasize the goal of economic self-sufficiency. Ultimately, how a funder evaluates a literacy program is instrumental in whether or not it is actually implemented and continued. In this way, funders influence the design of literacy programs and in so doing set literacy agendas for language minorities.

Funders, however, are not the only individuals involved in literacy programs. Teachers and students are also important stakeholders in literacy programs. How might teachers evaluate the programs described? In terms of the one-to-one programs, teachers in Help a Friend Learn English may like the existence of prepared materials. Teachers in the Action for Literacy program, although they may like the flexibility of the program in meeting students' individual needs, may find that the program requires a good deal of work because teachers need to select specific materials for each of their students. In terms of the group programs, teachers may or may not like the social consciousness component of the Focus on Change program, depending on their personal and educational philosophy. Teachers, then, may evaluate programs on dimensions quite different from those of funders or researchers.

How would learners assess the programs? This greatly depends on who the learner is and what his or her needs are at the time. Minh, Carlos, and Melchora, all of whom have literacy goals related to the workplace, will find Help a Friend Learn English unsuitable. Maria, however, who is less concerned with workplace skills, may find it appealing because of its bilingual component, its flexibility in time, and its location. On the other hand, Minh, Carlos, and Melchora may all find the inclusion of work skills appealing in the Action for Literacy program. Hoa, although not attracted to the workplace component Action for Literacy, may find its tutoring aspect desirable because of her shyness and the fact that she has child-care considerations. Hoa might also like the Vietnamese refugee program because it could answer concerns she might have about the country and the community. This program, however, would not meet the needs of Minh who has specific technical literacy goals. The Focus on Change program, although perhaps appealing to Melchora because of its attention to work skills and concern with sole-support mothers, may be impossible for her to attend if its set schedule of classes does not suit her work schedule. Also its philosophy may or may not be appealing to her. Each learner, then, has his or her own set of criteria by which to evaluate a program. To the extent that different interest groups evaluate programs by different standards, whose standards should apply in the evaluation of second language literacy programs?

In trying to incorporate the perspectives of all interested groups in program evaluation, Lytle and Wolfe (1989) set forth a model for adult literacy program evaluation that includes, among other things, the following features that they consider critical for program evaluation. First, they believe that program evaluation should be undertaken both within the program by staff and learners as well as by external evaluators. According to Lytle and Wolfe (1989), the value of external evaluators is that they can serve as "organizational anthropologists," who seek to understand the program from the perspectives of the staff, participants, and other groups affected by the program (p. 61). In this way they can bring needed expertise to the evaluation process. Lytle and Wolfe also advocate that learners as well as staff members be involved in internal program evaluation, particularly because they are the most important stakeholders of all the interest groups involved. Furthermore, they maintain that the standards by which programs are evaluated should be generated from literacy theory, research, and program practice. These standards should be explicitly stated so that evaluators can determine what practices meet these standards. Finally, Lytle and Wolfe argue that program evaluation should involve critical reflection on the philosophy and goals of the program by all interested parties. Because the concept of success and definitions of literacy can differ among administrators, teachers, learners, and funders, Lytle and Wolfe believe such reflection can help to understand the discrepancies in evaluation among these different interest groups. This model provides an excellent basis on which to undertake a program evaluation process that includes the perspectives of all the major stakeholders in a literacy program.

Program implementation

In light of the fact that researchers, funders, teachers, and learners may employ different criteria in evaluating programs, some of which conflict with each other, whose standards will likely be adopted in implementing a program? Most likely there will be some negotiating of goals and standards in the process of designing and implementing a program, although ultimately those with the most power will have their goals and standards met. Often these are the program's funders, whose goals can be influenced by a variety of factors. If funders wish to meet the needs of program participants, they may seek out opinions from teachers and learners in the communities about their goals. They may, however, face difficulties in getting input from learners because of such factors as a lack of contact with community leaders, a lack of English language proficiency on the part of the learners with no bilingual support available, or cross-cultural communication problems. Perhaps it is for these reasons that Wrigley (1991), as was mentioned earlier, found very few literacy programs that involved learners in overall program design. Thus, the most important stakeholders in second language literacy programs often do not have their literacy agendas heard. In addition, funders may face budgetary constraints that make it difficult to enact the type of program they might like to see. Furthermore, funders may be answerable to outside influences such as taxpayers and boards of directors who do not support their objectives for literacy programs. Because of factors such as these, actual literacy program designs may fall short of what funders and participants desire.

Literacy programs set literacy agendas through such factors as their overall program goals, be they individually oriented or community-oriented, and through the standards they employ in evaluating the program. They can also limit the learning options that are available to language minorities through such program features as high tuition fees and inconvenient scheduling and location. Literacy programs, however, are not the only way educational literacy agendas are set. Literacy agendas are also enacted through literacy curricula. In order to illustrate what forces are operative in the implementation of literacy curricula, we turn now to a discussion of various models of curriculum design.

Second language literacy curriculum

Curriculum orientations

In an overview of second language literacy curricula, Wrigley and Guth (1992) distinguish six basic orientations to literacy curricula, each based on a particular view of language, literacy, and learning. In addition they point out the possible drawbacks of each orientation. As a basis for discussing how curriculum designers set literacy agendas, we review these orientations.

The first one, the *development of cognitive processes* orientation, emphasizes "learning how to learn," stressing process over content, as well as strategies over skills, and understanding rather than memorization. In a literacy class, such a curriculum would include activities such as predicting meaning from context and using one's general knowledge to understand a text. Problem-solving strategies would also be emphasized. Critics, however, argue that this orientation ignores issues of the wider society, separating learning from social action.

The second orientation, *common educational core,* reflects a view of literacy as a common core of knowledge and skills, an idea most recently expressed in the United States in Hirsch's (1987) widely cited work, *Cultural Literacy: What Every American Needs to Know,* in which literacy, in addition to the acquisition of reading and writing skills, is viewed as the acquisition of a body of favored knowledge. Within this orientation, second language literacy curricula teach basic skills, including phonics, punctuation, and correct interpretation of a reading passage, using content that focuses on traditional cultural values. Critics of this orientation maintain that it is ethnocentric in its promotion of traditional cultural values. Furthermore, Wrigley and Guth argue that it can promote a deficit model of literacy, in which language minority families are seen as lacking in linguistic skills and cultural knowledge.

The third orientation delineated by Wrigley and Guth is *personal relevance.* This orientation emphasizes the primacy of personal meaning in second language literacy and results in a curriculum that focuses on the affective dimension of reading and writing and sees personal growth as one of its main objectives. It supports the idea that adults are able to assess their own literacy needs. Critics maintain that this approach, like the cognitive processes orientation, has an individual orientation and thus fails to address broader economic and political issues.

The fourth orientation, *social adaptation,* is designed to help learners acquire the skills and knowledge needed to be self-sufficient and function effectively in the society. Curricula reflecting such an orientation have clearly specified objectives based on tasks that students need to perform in the larger society. The goals of such curricula are clearly articulated and performance based; in refugee education these goals often are specified as life skills designed to help individuals find work and maintain jobs. Critics maintain that the orientation reflects a "factory model to literacy," in which literacy is limited to work-related skills.

The issues of culture and power form the basis for the fifth orientation, the *social change* orientation. In the tradition of Freire, the goal of this type of curriculum is to enable students to help bring about social change. In this orientation, literacy is viewed not as the cause of poverty or underemployment but as the result of social conditions that are inequitable. The orientation supports a participatory approach to curriculum development in that students specify the social issues they want to change. The program Focus on Change, which we examined earlier, exemplifies a curriculum based on this orientation. Critics of this orientation, however, argue that the approach is paternalistic and that it assumes that all language minorities feel oppressed and, therefore, desire to change the society.

Finally, the *curriculum as technology* orientation employs models borrowed from industry and uses terms such as training modules and literacy audits. Technology influences the entire literacy curriculum in that computer-designed programs move students through an instructional sequence and track their progress at each level. Such curricula are frequently used in workplace literacy programs. Critics of the approach reject what they see as an apolitical, unethical, and atheoretical orientation. Furthermore, some teacher educators maintain that the prepackaged programs will further undermine the professional status of teachers.

In supporting a particular orientation in their materials, curriculum designers set agendas for literacy classes. For example, if curriculum designers adopt a *social adaptation* orientation, their materials will include tasks such as filling out job applications or writing résumés. On the other hand, curriculum designers who support a *personal relevance* orientation will create materials that encourage students to do such things as write about their own life experiences and discuss their likes and dislikes.

Curriculum developers also set agendas by using particular content in their materials. Several curriculum theorists (Apple, 1979; Freire, 1970; Giroux, 1983) maintain that education is an important socializing agent. The content that a curriculum uses is important in defining social roles. For example, the following literacy text, through its choice of content, could be viewed as socializing students for very limited working-class roles:

1. Go to work on time. Don't be late. . . .
2. Work hard. Don't be lazy.

3. Work carefully. Always do your best.
4. Ask questions if you don't understand or are not sure . . .
5. Be friendly. Get along with everybody. Be nice to the other workers. .
. . Smile at them. Be clean and neat.

(Walsh, 1984, as cited in Auerbach, 1986, p. 418)

Whereas curricula such as these socialize students for limited roles in society, curriculum designers who adhere to a social change orientation strive in their content to change the social order. Thus, curriculum designers set agendas in their materials by supporting a particular social philosophy in which literacy can be viewed as a means for functioning in the society as it exists or for changing the social order.

Curriculum selection

A variety of forces, however, affects the ultimate selection of a literacy curriculum orientation for use in a particular educational setting. One factor is the need for accountability. In the United States in the 1980s, many adult second language literacy programs were competency-based, employing what Wrigley and Guth (1992) term a social adaptation curriculum orientation. Such curricula were based on a performance-based outline of language tasks believed to be necessary for adults to function in society (Auerbach, 1986, p. 413). These curricula were adopted largely because various funding sources at the time mandated that programs use competency-based curricula. During this period, for example, the U.S. government mandated that any refugee who wished to receive federal assistance for education had to be enrolled in a competency-based program (Auerbach, 1986, p. 412). One reason funders endorsed competency-based curricula was that the goals of the curriculum were clearly specified in behavioral terms and thus relatively easy to test. These test scores provided them with some means of accountability. In this way, the need to be accountable to funders through some objective measurement is one factor that can influence whether or not a particular curriculum orientation is adopted.

Another factor that can affect the selection of one curriculum design over another is the issue of cost. All of the curriculum orientations described in the preceding section differ in the amount of teacher training required to use them and the cost of teaching materials, two components that have an impact on the overall cost of their implementation. Adopting a curriculum such as technology orientation, for example, could be expensive because it requires both computers and software. On the other hand, in evaluating the Laubach materials for a

Canadian context, Read and Mackay (1984, p. 89) point out that this curriculum may be appealing primarily because of its cost effectiveness. Because the Laubach organization supplies a full range of student and teacher books, along with a program that trains teachers in a very short time, "the start-up costs are minimised" and thus may be attractive to funders and administrators. Cost, then, is another factor that may affect which curriculum is ultimately selected.

A final factor that can influence the selection of a curriculum is the evaluation of a curriculum by educators. To the extent that educators are consulted, their opinions can influence the choice of a curriculum. Although educators may not share the standards of accountability and cost used by funders, they nevertheless have their own standards by which to judge a curriculum. Often their standards are based on a particular educational philosophy involving beliefs about how language is learned and what role teachers and students should have in the educational process. Such standards are evident in Read and Mackay's (1984) evaluation of the Language Experience Approach for a Canadian context. The Language Experience approach exemplifies what Wrigley and Guth (1992) term a *personal relevance* orientation. It begins with a discussion of the participants' common interests or problems. This is followed by an attempt to write a group account of the discussion. The teacher acts as a recorder, transcribing exactly what the students say on the board. This text then becomes a reading text that forms the basis for further literacy activities.

Read and Mackay (1984) rate this approach very highly for a variety of reasons. First, it supports a view of literacy learning that they consider sound. As they point out, by presenting language in context, it supports the view that language is a meaningful whole (Read & Mackay, 1984, p. 91). In addition, by not correcting errors in the student-generated text, it supports the notion that errors are a natural part of the learning process and should not be emphasized when the focus is on meaning. Second, the curriculum supports their belief that curriculum content should be relevant to the learners and based on their needs. Third, the curriculum supports a role of the learner as being able to guide course content rather than having the content dictated by the teacher. Finally, the curriculum necessitates a trained and flexible teacher, a factor that they believe is highly desirable. In this way, their evaluation of the curriculum is based on their own literacy education philosophy. To the extent that their views are sought in the selection of literacy curriculum, they set agendas for literacy education. These are some of the forces that can influence the ultimate selection of a curriculum in a particular educational setting. However, the extent to which the curriculum that is selected is actually implemented in the classroom is another matter.

Curriculum implementation

Who controls the implementation of a curriculum: curriculum designers, teachers, students, or some combination of these individuals? Auerbach (1990, pp. 51–52) distinguishes two types of curriculum control: the ends-means approach and the participatory approach. In the former, curriculum development starts with a group of experts identifying a body of knowledge to be covered. Often in determining the content to be covered, curriculum designers consult those in the mainstream society who will be interacting with the learners to see what expectations they have for the learners. Employers, for example, might be asked what literacy tasks they expect of their workers. In this way, the content of the curriculum is derived from an externally defined body of knowledge. In addition, needs assessment is often done *a priori* as a precondition for instruction. In implementing the curriculum, the teacher's role is to transmit the content specified in the curriculum to the students.

On the other hand, in the participatory approach, the curriculum develops from the needs and interests of the learners. Needs assessment is an ongoing process, integrated into the classroom interaction. The teacher's role is to act as a problem poser who tries to determine what curriculum content will meet the needs of the learners. In short, the learning process is a collective endeavor. The teacher's role is to draw out the participation of the students in order to define issues and activities to be dealt with in the class (Auerbach, 1990, pp. 54–55).

These models characterize idealized types of curriculum control. When a curriculum is actually implemented in a classroom, however, it may be that, rather than curriculum control reflecting one model or the other, classroom interaction may actually exemplify an ends-means approach or a participatory approach to a greater or lesser extent, depending on the teacher and students. Whereas teachers and tutors in programs such as Help a Friend Learn English are given a set curriculum, the enactment of this curriculum likely involves an ongoing negotiation between teachers and students. To a great degree, who controls the enactment of a curriculum depends on the relationship that exists between a teacher and a group of learners. Furthermore, who sets the curriculum agenda may vary within a period of time. Thus, initially some teachers may encourage a great deal of student participation, but this initial participation could then result in an ends-means curriculum. On the other hand, some teachers may encourage participation throughout a literacy course.

In some cases, then, students such as the Trans, the Cierras, and the Galangs will find that they are asked to direct the curriculum based on their needs and interests. In other cases, however, the teacher will largely determine what they study. Rarely, however, will the choice of approach be theirs. Rather, this choice will ultimately be in the hands of teachers who hold a particular educational philosophy or in the hands of funders and administrators who must face cost and accountability issues or in the hands of curriculum designers who have certain beliefs about the role of student participation.

If, however, learners such as Hoa, Minh, Maria, Carlos, and Melchora were to implement a curriculum to meet their needs, what might it look like? In all probability, it would not fall neatly into one of the orientations described earlier; rather, it would draw from several orientations and change over time as their literacy needs and personal and family needs changed. For example, whereas at some point, Carlos may want a curriculum with a social adaptation orientation in order to pass an amnesty test, later he might want a technology-based orientation to attain specific job skills. At other times, dissatisfied with social and economic conditions, he may want a literacy curriculum that addresses issues of social change. One of the major problems with implementing a curriculum that would meet Carlos's needs has to do with issues of cost and feasibility. Even in a one-to-one context, such a curriculum would demand highly trained teachers and a diverse set of teaching materials, factors that involve high costs that generally have not been forthcoming in many Anglophone countries. Fingeret (1984, p. 18), for example, points out that in the United States, although the federally initiated National Adult Literacy Project advocated volunteer efforts in adult literacy education that would provide one-to-one literacy training, it did not provide the resources essential for effective training and use of volunteers.

Cost and feasibility are not the only factors that can limit the enactment of a curriculum that best meets the needs and desires of language minorities. Another restriction has to do with issues of accountability. In order to demonstrate how issues of accountability affect educational literacy agendas, we turn now to a discussion of literacy assessment.

Second language literacy assessment

Assessment versus evaluation

Evaluation and assessment are often distinguished. Shaw and Dowsett (1986), for example, distinguish assessment and evaluation in the following manner:

Assessment refers to the practices of and procedures for measuring individual student performance in an educational activity. This may include formal measures, e.g. proficiency ratings and informal measures such as checklists of skills learnt. . . .

Evaluation refers to the practices and procedures for measuring the effectiveness of a course or program of study offered to students in any educational institution. Evaluation is a process of reflection on those practices and procedures for the purpose of decision-making. (p. 10)

Whereas in our previous discussion of literacy programs and curriculum, we were concerned with evaluation, in the following discussion we will focus on assessment. However, we will define assessment more broadly than did Shaw and Dowsett (1986). We will consider assessment not only in the context of the educational environment but also in the larger society. We will do this in order to illustrate how the second language literacy assessment procedures that exist on various levels of society serve different purposes.

As was pointed out in previous chapters, literacy assessment exists in various arenas of the society. Countries can undertake literacy assessment in order to document the state of literacy in the nation. Industries can employ literacy assessment procedures as part of their professional certification requirements. Educators too can undertake assessment to accomplish such tasks as placing students in courses and determining the areas in which students need further instruction. On one level, the purpose of these assessment procedures is to make decisions. National leaders may want to know the extent of illiteracy, as they define it, in order to make decisions about possible ways to deal with the so-called literacy problem. Industrial leaders may want to know what literacy skills individuals have in order to decide whether or not to certify them. Educators may want to know whether students can complete certain literacy tasks in order to make decisions about future instruction.

On another level, however, assessment procedures can serve other agendas. National leaders may undertake assessment procedures to convince taxpayers that there is a literacy problem in order to secure their financial support. Industrial leaders may use assessment procedures to restrict entry to the professions, thus protecting the interests of those who are already employed. Educators may undertake assessment to convince funding sources that their money is being well used.

Literacy assessment on a national level

In order to illustrate the many purposes that assessment can serve, we will begin by discussing a case of literacy assessment on a national level. In doing so we will demonstrate the fact that who is assessing literacy and what their purpose is determines how literacy is defined and how it is measured. As Shaw and Dowsett (1986) point out, many individuals have a stake in assessment:

The students have a stake in their learning and in obtaining appropriate teaching; the teachers have a stake in ensuring that their teaching is assisted by any evaluation procedures to become more effective; administrators need to ensure that effective teaching and learning are taking place and that the policies which guide the educative process are sound, supportive and efficient. (p. 113)

Added to this list of stakeholders can be government officials who may want certain policies endorsed as well as funders and taxpayers who may want some type of evidence that their money is being used productively. These are the stakeholders that were served by a recent effort to assess literacy in Australia.

The Australian government's endorsement of a National Policy on Languages included a recommendation for an Adult Literacy Action Campaign. One of the features of this campaign was to generate information regarding the issue of literacy in Australia through a "detailed co-ordinated national level collection of both quantitative and qualitative information" (lo Bianco, 1987, as cited in Wickert, 1989, p. 1). The purpose of assessing literacy on a national basis was to persuade government officials and taxpayers of the existence of a literacy problem in Australia so that funding for literacy would continue (Wickert, 1989, p. 1). As part of an effort to document the extent of the problem, a study was sponsored by the Department of Employment, Education, and Training and published under the title *No Single Measure,* capturing the idea that there is no single measure which separates literates from illiterates. Nevertheless, central to the study was the development of a tool to assess literacy on a numerical basis.

In the study, literacy was viewed as "a set of skills that people have to varying degrees. Their ability to use these skills may vary from one context to another" (Wickert, 1989, p. 4). The research design adopted in the study followed the strategy used by the Educational Testing Service of the United States in their National Assessment of Educational Progress (NAEP) literacy survey of young adults, in which simulations of literacy tasks were used to assess literacy. Viewing literacy as a set of skills that vary from context to context and that individuals possess to varying degrees, the researchers in *No Single Measure* set about developing simulation tasks of various skills at various levels. The tasks included in the survey were categorized into one of three types: document literacy, prose literacy, and quantitative literacy. By using and analyzing different kinds of literacy tasks at different levels of complexity, the researchers argued that the test allowed for "the possibility of developing profiles not only of a person's literacy proficiencies but also of the literacy requirements of, say, particular occupations" (Wickert, 1989, p. 4).

Simulation tasks were developed to represent a variety of purposes people have for using printed material, including such tasks as locating specific information, following instructions to make or repair something, and using printed information to compare points of view. A variety of printed material was also used, including such documents as signs, forms, bills, invoices, advertisements, timetables, graphs, and charts (Wickert, 1989, p. 7). In the area of document literacy, individuals were asked, for example, to write out a check, fill out a job application form, identify the gross pay on a paycheck, or read a map (Wickert, 1989, p. 12). In the area of prose literacy, students were given a piece of prose and asked to locate information in the text, produce and interpret text information, and determine a theme or organizing principle from the text (Wickert, 1989, p. 17). In the area of quantitative literacy, individuals were asked to complete such tasks as figuring the surcharge on a menu or reading an airline schedule (Wickert, 1989, p. 22). The test was administered to 1500 adults aged 18 and over with the results reported on a five-point scale: advanced, adept, intermediate, basic, and rudimentary, based on the number of tasks an individual was able to successfully perform.

Instructive for our purposes are the findings of the study in regard to the nonnative English-speaking test takers. In comparison with the native speakers of English, the nonnative English-speaking group, not surprisingly, performed at a lower level. What is interesting, however, is the types of tasks on which they tended to do poorly. The three tasks on which there was the greatest difference were writing checks on a charge card, giving past details on a job application form, and reading a prose passage on technology in Australia. There were also large differences in such tasks as identifying the gross pay to date on a pay slip, putting the cash entry on a deposit slip, calculating change for a restaurant charge, and reading a flight schedule from Brisbane (Wickert, 1989, p. 30). Many of the tasks, then, that were difficult for the nonnative English speakers necessitated knowledge of Australia and of middle-class life. Little, however, is made of this fact in the study. Rather, the results were analyzed in relation to other variables such as the amount of English used by individuals in childhood and their age and length of residence in Australia. The study, for example, found that there was no "evidence that literacy in English improves with length of residence in Australia" (Wickert, 1989, p. 36).

Although the results of the study meet the agenda of documenting the extent of illiteracy in Australia (as literacy is defined in the study), a recognition of their significance can be lost in citing the results. Why, for example, does English literacy in Australia, as measured by the test, not increase in relation to the length of time a nonnative speaker lives there? Why do the nonnative English-speaking test takers not do as well on items related to bureaucracy and finances as do other Australians? But most important, if as Shaw and Dowsett (1986, p. 112) point out, one of the primary purposes of assessment is the "retrieval of information for decision making," what does the information obtained through such a study, given the instrument used, suggest about decision making and future assessment in reference to second language literacy?

Certainly the results suggest that cultural knowledge affected the scores of nonnative speakers of English on the test. One implication of this fact is that test designers must consider to what extent they believe cultural knowledge should be relevant to the assessment of English literacy. As has been pointed out throughout the book, the extent to which English literacy should include a cultural component is a matter that should be explicitly addressed rather than assumed. In reporting test results, designers should make explicit their assumptions in this regard and evaluate the results of the test in this light.

In addition, the fact that scores on the test did not increase in relation to the length of time language minority individuals lived in Australia is one that merits attention. One decision that could develop from this finding is to examine the reasons for this situation. What factors in the social, economic, and educational context of the country are preventing language minorities from developing English literacy practices, at least as they are measured on the test? Finally and perhaps most importantly, before tests such as those reported on in *No Single Measure* are used to document the state of illiteracy among language minorities, it is essential that the findings be consistently qualified as "not literate in English" and that such findings be supplemented with information on the extent of literacy in the mother tongue. Doing so would provide a much more valid picture of the state of literacy among language minorities.

In the case of the research study, *No Single Measure,* some of the primary stakeholders who were being served were government and educational leaders who wanted to convince taxpayers of the need to continue to use their taxes to address the problem of adult illiteracy in Australia. Although those who took the test would seem to also be stakeholders in the process, their purposes are served only to the extent that the findings of the study result in decisions that will be beneficial to them. If the results do not lead to such decisions, the test has done little to meet their needs even though the assessment procedure has met the needs of government and educational leaders. The possible failure of literacy assessment procedures to meet the needs of second language learners does not exist only on a national level. It can also occur in educational settings.

Literacy assessment in an educational context

One group of stakeholders in the process of literacy assessment in an educational context is program administrators. In order to continue getting funding for their programs, program administrators often need to document that effective teaching and learning are taking place. One way they frequently accomplish this task is through the use of standardized tests similar to those described in the preceding section. Many standardized tests exist to document adult basic skills, for example, the Test of Adult Basic Education and the Basic English Skills Test in the United States. Generally these tests use a paper-and-pencil format with multiple-choice or fill-in-the-blank questions that focus on decontextualized word recognition and sentence or paragraph comprehension skills, reflecting a skill-based view of literacy. Why is such a view of literacy employed and why are such tests used?

From a program administrator's point of view, standardized tests that assess discrete literacy skills have several advantages. They are easily scored and thus are cost effective. In addition, they allow for comparison of data across programs, and they can provide feedback to students who want to know how they are doing in comparison to other students. Perhaps because of these advantages, Balliro (1989), in a survey of teachers, administrators, and funders of adult ESL programs in northwestern United States, found that, owing to external demands for standardized measurements of progress, most programs assessed students either through standardized tests or performance standards. In fact, according to Auerbach (1990), current second language literacy assessment in the United States can be characterized as one of "accountability through quantification" (p. 206).

Although such procedures may meet the needs of administrators, the learners themselves are also central stakeholders in the assessing of second language literacy. Do such tests meet their assessment needs? According to Auerbach (1990, pp. 207–209), standardized tests do little to meet the needs of second language learners. In fact, she contends that they may negatively influence the literacy learning process because of drawbacks such as the following. First, the standardized test process itself can be intimidating and demeaning. For many adults, test taking can be stressful; in addition, some of the tests used are adapted from tests for middle-class children and include questions on such topics as farm animals and birds in the park. Second, framing the results in terms of grade levels can be destructive. When adults are told "that their performance is comparable to second or third graders, much more is being communicated than an objective description of ability" (Lytle, 1988, p. 2). Third, because the concept and content of standardized tests are culture specific, second language learners are often asked to deal with what is for them culturally unfamiliar material.

In addition, for Auerbach (1990), many standardized tests measure the wrong things and fail to measure the right ones. Because it is easier to tabulate discrete answers, standardized tests often focus on isolated skills (such as letter and word recognition) rather than on assessing other aspects of literacy (such as critical thinking or creativity). Furthermore, they don't provide information about affective factors related to literacy acquisition, such as the influence of literacy on students' personal growth or family life. Finally, and perhaps most important, testing shapes teaching. As Auerbach (1990) points out, "despite teachers' best intentions, the tail wags the dog – if program evaluation is based on test performance, inevitably, curricula are geared toward teaching to the tests. Since the tests generally measure subskills, this is what gets taught" (p. 209).

Although standardized tests then can serve the testing agendas of program administrators, they may negatively affect what they are intended to assess, namely, an individual's progress in acquiring second language literacy. They do this largely by viewing literacy solely as skill based. As Lytle, Belzer, Shultz, and Vannozzi (1989) put it, standardized tests often "fail to capture the richness and complexity of adult learning, and they reinforce a view of literacy as a set of autonomous, technical skills divorced from meaningful contexts" (p. 54). As was pointed out earlier, however, some educators view literacy not as a set of discrete skills but rather as a strategy-based process by which individuals learn how to do new things. For these educators, the challenge is to design measurements that can assess what they see as literacy in such a way that they can be accountable to funders.

In attempting to meet this challenge, Lytle et al. (1989, p. 55) describe a learner-centered or participatory approach to assessment. This approach is based on several assumptions, "among them that adults come to programs with particular goals, with previous experiences with literacy and with perceptions of reading, writing, and learning that all affect what and how they learn." Lytle et al. identify four dimensions of literacy learning that they believe should form the basis for literacy assessment. They term these practices, strategies and interests, perceptions, and goals. In the area of practices, they maintain that the assessment process should include having learners describe the various settings in which they engage in literacy practices. The home, community, and work environments of individuals should be explored in order to understand the social networks and contexts in which learners use or want to use literacy. To assess the strategies and interests of learners, Lytle et al. suggest giving learners a variety of literacy texts and tasks. How students deal with these would be documented in a portfolio of literacy activities compiled for each individual learner. In the area of perceptions, Lytle et al. suggest that the learners' theories of reading and writing, including their own learning history, should be explored and documented through interviews. And finally, in the area of goals, Lytle et al. suggest that learners "identify, prioritize and discuss their goals and purpose for literacy learning" (p. 56). These goals could be documented through checklists and interviews, for example.

In trying to implement such a participatory approach to literacy assessment in the Center for Literacy in Philadelphia, Lytle et al. (1989, p. 54) note several problems that arose. First, because adult learners are encouraged to take an active role in their own assessment procedures, these procedures can cause conflicts by creating new roles and power relationships for the staff and student. Second, some of the procedures used, such as interviews and collecting portfolios of students' literacy activities, were much more time-consuming than traditional standardized testing and, therefore, resisted by some staff members. And finally, because of the complex nature of this kind of assessment, staff members need more training in using them than is required in simply administering standardized tests. In light of these difficulties in implementation, Lytle et al. found that the staff itself became divided over the role of assessment. Whereas some staff members saw a participatory approach to literacy assessment as a means of helping adults become more active participants in their own learning, others viewed parts of the approach, such as the interviews, as "unnecessarily intrusive and a violation of personal privacy" (p. 63).

Although the learner-centered assessment advocated by Lytle et al. (1989) allows for a view of literacy as more than skill based and involves learners in their own assessment, its actual implementation will likely rest on whether staff resistance to its procedures can be overcome. Even more important, its implementation will depend on whether it can be documented in such a manner as to satisfy various stakeholders in assessment (such as funders and administrators). However, regardless of what type of assessment measures are used – standardized tests or learner-centered assessment – if the procedures do not result in decision making that in the long run contributes to learners' progress in literacy, the measures have not met one of the primary purposes of assessment.

If Hoa, Minh, Carlos, Maria, and Melchora were to assess their own literacy learning for their own purposes, what measures might they use? What was assessed would likely vary depending on the context. On a personal level, the ability to read an English newspaper or enjoy a story in English may be one measurement of success that they consider important. In a family context, being able to read a school bulletin in English may for them be another sign of progress. In an educational context, being able to write an essay or complete a grammar worksheet may be an indication of their progress. Finally, in an economic context, being able to pass a test for professional certification may be for them an important sign of their progress. Although learner-centered assessment procedures allow for such attainments to demonstrate learner progress, as we have seen, the implementation of such procedures faces several major obstacles.

Summary and implications

In this chapter we have examined how educational institutions can set second language literacy agendas through program and curriculum design. We have seen how literacy programs can vary in design and how they can be evaluated. Whereas funders may assess a program on its cost-effectiveness, program administrators may be concerned with issues such as staffing and material requirements. On the other hand, teachers may evaluate a program on how well it meets their views of education and literacy. Learners also have their own criteria, desiring programs that suit their literacy goals as well as their schedule and financial limitations. Whose agendas are implemented in program design will depend on a variety of factors, including the important considerations of the availability of funding.

We have also examined how second language literacy agendas are set through the design, selection, and implementation of a curriculum. We have seen how curriculum designers set literacy agendas in the curriculum orientation and the content they select. We have also considered how factors such as accountability, cost, and educational evaluation can affect whether a particular curriculum is selected for use in a program. In addition, we have explored how curricula are actually implemented in a classroom as teachers and students exert control over its implementation.

Finally, we have examined how literacy assessment can be used on various levels in society to meet different agendas. We have demonstrated that who is assessing literacy and for what reason affects how literacy is assessed. We have also discussed the various stakeholders in the assessment process and illustrated how their agendas can compete with one another. We have suggested that these competing agendas can undermine one of the most important reasons for literacy assessment, namely, to make decisions that are beneficial to language minorities so that they can attain their own literacy goals.

What does this discussion of literacy programs, curricula, and assessment suggest for second language literacy educators and program funders? First, the way a program is evaluated depends to a great degree on who is evaluating the program, so it is important for educators and funders to specify the criteria by which they are evaluating a program. They should also consult learners as to their criteria for evaluating a program both before the program is implemented and as part of an ongoing program evaluation. Because educators, funders, and learners all bring to literacy programs different interests, there will quite likely be differences in how they evaluate a particular program. What is important is that all interested parties specify their criteria for evaluation so that when there are competing criteria (as between a desire for cost efficiency and a desire for highly trained staff), these differences can be discussed and compromises reached. By undertaking this process, those with a vested interest in implementing literacy programs can better understand the perspectives that various individuals bring to the program.

Second, in the area of curriculum design and implementation, language minority students have very different literacy needs and goals that change over time, so literacy curricula will need to be varied and respond to students' literacy goals at the time. Implementing such a curriculum will necessitate educators who are familiar with various literacy orientations, textbooks, and materials. They will need to be able to draw on these resources to meet the needs of the learners, striving to balance the interests and needs of various students in the program with their own teaching preferences and ideologies. This is a difficult task, one that will require teachers to have a thorough understanding of sound literacy theory and practice, to be well informed on literacy curricula, and to constantly seek an understanding of the literacy needs of their students in their personal lives and communities.

Finally, in the area of assessment, the different purposes that tests can serve raise important issues. One common purpose of tests is to sort individuals into groups as is done in some national studies that attempt to document the extent of literacy in a country. One danger with such tests is that they may suggest that literacy is an either-or proposition rather than a continuum of practices. As was pointed out in Chapter 1, employing an either-or dichotomy presents a tremendous oversimplification of the concept of literacy. A second danger with such tests is that, by focusing exclusively on English literacy, they may suggest that this is the only literacy of value. Another common purpose of assessment is to document progress. When assessment measures are used for this purpose, the difficult question is to determine what should constitute progress. As with program evaluation, educators, funders, and learners are likely to have different answers to this question. In the process of answering the question and reaching a compromise, it may well be that the agreed-upon procedures for assessing progress will be time-consuming because they are individualized and document various measures of progress.

Throughout the book we have examined the literacy agendas that exist in various contexts – the sociopolitical, economic, family, and educational. As we have seen, the agendas that exist in these various domains can conflict with one another and, in so doing, can undermine the literacy goals of language minorities themselves. If, as educators, our objective is to help language minorities attain their own literacy goals, we need to ask what agendas we should set. It is this question that we turn to now.

6 Agendas for second language literacy

Minh is now able to read and write quite well in English. He is unhappy, however, because he has been unable to pass all the tests that are included in the medical technologist certification process. Both Hoa and Lan can read only a few words in English. They depend on Minh for most of their literacy needs. Neither of them is concerned about their lack of English literacy because they can function quite well as it is now. Even with no English literacy, Lan is pleased that her business (selling locally made crafts) is doing very well. Carlos is able to read and write well enough in English so that he was able to pass the test required for naturalization. Now he would like to improve his reading and writing for job purposes and union activities. He feels that his lack of English literacy abilities is keeping him from being promoted; he also believes that, if his writing were better, he might be able to enlist the help of the union in getting English literacy classes for language minorities as part of their workday. Maria has gained some ability in reading and writing in English, but she would like to improve so that she can read for her own enjoyment and help her children with their schoolwork. Often she is embarrassed when she can't help her children with their school reading and writing assignments. Melchora can read simple things in English, such as directions or warnings that she has encountered at the various places where she has worked. She is frustrated that she cannot afford the time to study English because she believes that, if she were able to do this, she could get a better job and send more money home to her children.

Literacy as a problem

As we have seen throughout the book, many forces have influenced the literacy agendas of these individuals. The desire of professional leaders to establish standards for their profession as well as to limit entry

125

to the profession has affected Minh's second language literacy agenda. The decision of political leaders to enact literacy requirements for naturalization and citizenship for the purpose of national unity as well as to encourage assimilation has affected Carlos's second language literacy agenda. The decision of political and educational leaders to designate a medium of instruction in the schools, often out of a desire for efficiency, as well as to encourage assimilation has affected the second language literacy agendas of the children in these families. In so doing, the decision has influenced the families' agendas for literacy and at times negatively affected the dynamics of the family. In many instances, in enacting such literacy policies, political, economic, and educational leaders view individuals such as the Trans, the Cierras, and the Galangs as part of a national literacy "problem" that can undermine the unity and economic development of the country. When families such as the Trans, the Cierras, and the Galangs are viewed as a problem, certain questions are asked. We turn now to a consideration of some of the questions that arise in adopting a problem-solution framework and challenge this framework as a productive approach to second language literacy.

Is illiteracy a problem?

One important question that arises in viewing these individuals as part of a national literacy problem is whether there actually is a literacy problem. As we have pointed out, many Anglophone countries have launched literacy campaigns in which national leaders argue that illiteracy is widespread and that the lack of literacy abilities among many in the country will eventually lead to the economic decline of the country. Yet there are others who argue that this so-called literacy problem is to some extent a fabrication. Some argue that the standardized tests used to assess the extent of literacy in a country are often tautological since the competencies they define as necessary for success are the very ones they use as measures on the test. Furthermore, they contend that standardized tests that require both silent reading and the ability to read unfamiliar material are "relatively new ways of assessing and thus defining literacy. As a result, the nation perceives itself as having a literacy crisis because its expectations about literacy are . . . different in quality than they have been in the past" (Gowen, 1990, pp. 67–68).

Some contend that there has not been a decline in literacy within Anglophone nations but a change in the expectations of literacy levels. Rose (1989), for example, points out that:

Statistics are often used to demonstrate educational decay, but let's consider our literacy crisis through the perspective provided by another set of numbers. In 1890, 6.7 percent of American's fourteen- to seventeen-year-olds were attending high school; by 1978 the number had risen to 94.1 percent. In the 1930s "functional literacy" was defined . . . as a state of having three or more years of schooling . . . by the late 1970s some authorities were suggesting that completion of high school should be the defining criterion of functional literacy. (as cited in Gowen, 1990, p. 67)

Some even contend that the so-called literacy problem is in essence "a way of sorting people into groups or castes" (Gowen, 1990, p. 69). Mikulecky (1990), for example, argues that "because literacy use and purpose are so closely linked with racially segregated social contexts and networks, a heavy potential exists that literacy may be used inappropriately for discrimination and gatekeeping" (p. 29). There are those then who seriously question whether or not there is a literacy problem. However, when a problem-solution framework is adopted, another question arises, namely, who should be included in the problem?

Who should be included?

In an assessment of national literacy, many members of the Tran, the Cierra, and the Galang families would probably be considered to be part of the problem. Just who would be counted as part of this problem would depend on how literacy was measured. If grade-level attainment were used, all of them might be considered as part of the problem. If standardized tests were used, who would be counted would depend on each one's score and on the kind of cutoff point used for establishing literacy. In any case, however, it is quite likely that Hoa, who can read and write only a few words in English, would be considered as part of the problem even though she is literate in her native language.

Yet if her native language literacy were taken into account, this could make a significant difference in national figures on illiteracy rates. Wiley (1991), for example, points out that in one survey of Chicanos in the United States, if only English literacy had been measured, illiteracy would have been 48 percent, whereas it would have been 26 percent if Spanish literacy had been included. Such findings demonstrate the importance of expanding the notion of literacy in Anglophone countries. To limit literacy to English literacy exclusively exaggerates the extent of the problem and inaccurately labels many individuals as not literate when in fact they are literate in their mother tongue. Another question that arises in adopting a problem-solution framework to literacy is whether illiteracy is the cause or the symptom of the problem.

Is illiteracy the cause or the symptom of the problem?

As was pointed out earlier, those who approach literacy as the cause of the problem frequently argue that if the problem of adult illiteracy is not dealt with, Anglophone countries will suffer a decline in productivity and be unable to compete in an international market. In short, illiteracy is viewed as the cause of the possible economic decline of the nation. On the other hand, there are those who argue that illiteracy is not the cause of the problem but rather the symptom of other social problems. Many adult illiterates do not view themselves as contributing to a problem but rather believe that they are in some sense a victim of the existing social structure. Gowen (1990), for example, points out that the research of World Education, a private organization which deals with nonschool literacy development, has shown that illiterate adults "rarely see their problem as one of literacy, but rather as a symptom of the condition of their lives in general" (p. 59).

Some argue that the literacy problem is, in fact, a symptom of problems in literacy training – problems that demand a restructuring of the educational system. Stuckey (1991), for example, argues that

we must understand the connections between literacy and economy, literacy and work, literacy and race, gender, class, literacy and English teachers. We must understand the extraordinary power of the educational process and of literacy standards not merely to exclude citizens from participating in the country's economic and political life but to brand them and their children with indelible prejudice, the prejudice of language. We must reform the educational process to demand diversity, to destroy . . . the myth that "excellence is impossible if there is diversity." (p. 122)

The question of whether illiteracy is the cause or the symptom of the problem has important implications for determining how to remedy the problem.

How can the problem be remedied?

Those who believe that individuals who are not literate are the cause of the problem contend that the remedy will depend on changes in the illiterate adults themselves as well as in the educational institutions that train them. Those who support this position promote a deficit model of illiterate adults, a view that unfortunately has widespread support. In fact, Gowen (1990, p. 72) points out that up until the early 1980s the majority of studies on illiterate adults supported a deficit model. Within this perspective, illiterate individuals are viewed as deficient in an important skill, and it is their responsibility, with the help of the school, to achieve the literacy skills necessary to remedy their deficiency. Frequently, those who see the individual and school as bearing the burden for solving the literacy problem also point to the failure of the schools to address the literacy demands of the current work force. They argue that schools need to promote a wider variety of contexts and uses of literacy than has traditionally been done so that students will be able to deal with the literacy demands of work. In general, as Mikulecky (1990) points out, they believe that "increasing and broadening school reading demands" is essential (p. 31).

On the other hand, those who reject the idea that the remedy depends solely on changes in the illiterate adult point out that many individuals who are not literate are often productive citizens and function quite well in the society. Mikulecky (1990), for example, contends that "it is inappropriate and inaccurate to assume that low literate adults are helpless in the face of generally high national literacy demands" (p. 28). Rather, research has shown such adults to be "intelligent, capable human beings able to function reasonably well in their own social networks." Furthermore, those who reject the remedy as lying with the individual argue that, although the educational structure may need to change to solve the illiteracy problem, ultimately the solution to a literacy problem will depend on changes in the overall social system. Fingeret (1984), for instance, in her assessment of adult literacy education, maintains:

It is important to remember that education will not create additional jobs, solve the problems of crime and malnutrition, or make the world safe from terrorism. Social structures and social forces beyond the reach of literacy educators are at work maintaining the structures of social inequality. Education can, however, provide tools and access to opportunities for working together with others to change those structures. (p. 45)

These are the questions that are considered and debated when literacy is approached as a problem. Adopting such a perspective can have two serious negative consequences. First, to the degree that the problem is seen to lie in the individual, such a perspective can marginalize individuals who are not literate, engendering negative social attitudes toward such individuals. Thus, Carlos and Melchora, because they are not highly literate in English, may be seen as less productive workers who limit the economic growth of the country. Or Alberto may be labeled as a problem in the school because he cannot read as well in English as his peers, leading, as Spener (1988) points out, to such children being seen as "imperfect or inferior members of the domestic culture" (p. 149). Second, a problem-solution framework, by demanding a cause and a remedy for the problem, can result in political and educational leaders pointing to each other as major contributors to the problem in their failure to address the problem. Political leaders can argue that schools are at fault for not providing adequate literacy training, whereas educational leaders point to the lack of economic support for adequate programs. In this way two major forces that should be working together to provide opportunities for literacy education become opposing factions.

If, however, one rejects the whole model of language minorities as being or having a problem because of their level of English literacy proficiency and examines instead what second language literacy agendas these individuals have and how they can be attained, different issues arise. Each of the adults in these three families has his or her own agenda for English literacy, even when it involves, as in the case of Hoa and Lan, not wanting to acquire English literacy. Both Hoa and Lan have productive lives without English literacy; they are able to interact in their families and their social network with Vietnamese and spoken English. They do not view themselves as having a problem. On the other hand, Minh, Carlos, Maria, and Melchora have literacy agendas that at the present time are unmet through no fault of their own. Rather than viewing them as having a literacy problem, the question that we need to ask is: What needs to be done for them to fulfill the second language literacy agendas they have?

Literacy agendas

A variety of groups would have to act in order to enable Minh, Carlos, Maria, and Melchora to meet their literacy goals: second language literacy educators, program administrators, program funders, and government leaders are some of these groups. The action of each group, however, would have to be based on the second language literacy agendas that language minorities themselves set because ultimately, "they are the most knowledgeable about the functions of literacy in their social contexts. More important, their lives and futures are being considered" (Fingeret, 1984, p. 43).

Although all of these groups would need to listen to the desires of the language minorities themselves, the leadership for helping them to attain their literacy agendas must come from literacy educators. "Literacy educators may look to policy makers for assistance, but they must look to each other for leadership" (Fingeret, 1984, p. 40). It is, after all, literacy educators – next to the language minorities themselves – who have the greatest interest in helping such individuals reach their second language literacy agendas because they are the ones held accountable for literacy education. What would literacy educators need to do to enable people such as the Trans, the Cierras, and the Galangs to attain their literacy goals?

Literacy programs

First, literacy educators would need to design and encourage a variety of literacy programs that could meet the individual needs of language minorities. For Minh, this might mean providing a specialized course dealing specifically with professional certification requirements. In addition, it might mean working with professional organizations or state regulatory agencies to design alternate literacy assessment measures for nonnative speakers of English that would reduce unnecessary culture-specific information and complex language in certification testing. For Carlos, it might mean designing a workplace literacy program that deals not just with job-related literacy skills but also with union advocacy. In order to do this, literacy educators may need to convince employers and labor leaders of the value of dealing with general workplace issues in the program.

For Maria, it might mean designing a family literacy program that will support her agenda to help her children in their school work, while never losing sight of the many parenting roles that Maria successfully undertakes without English literacy. Indeed, Maria can be a key figure in enabling her children to read and write in their mother tongue and become biliterate. In order to encourage this, literacy educators could work to see that Maria's ability to teach native language literacy is included in the program. For Melchora, it might mean designing a job-training program that has a flexible schedule. Furthermore, it might mean working with local labor leaders to find out what skills they are looking for in particular jobs so that the program can be geared to such skill development. In addition, literacy educators need to establish close links with employers so that Melchora would not only gain specific job-related skills but, in doing so, be assured of a job. In short, it will mean designing innovative programs that often are linked to the larger community.

Although the design of these programs will differ depending on the needs of the learners and the nature of the community, each of them should demonstrate the following characteristics, all of which develop from the discussions we have had throughout the book. In previous chapters we have demonstrated how various interest groups have different literacy agendas for language minorities and how those with the most power often have the greatest chance of having their agendas implemented. In light of this fact, it is essential that literacy programs be participatory in their design, implementation, and assessment. Being participatory in design means that funders, administrators, teachers, and, most importantly, language minorities all need to have input into program design. Typically, as Wrigley (1991) points out, it is on this level that there is the least learner input, yet it is precisely on this level that the greatest possibility exists for the development of programs that can meet the literacy needs of language minorities. A participatory approach also suggests that in the implementation the program, teachers, language minorities, and administrators need to work on an ongoing basis to have the classroom activities meet the literacy needs of the learners. Finally, a participatory approach, as was pointed out in Chapter 5, means that in the assessment process, measures of success should come not only from funders, administrators, and teachers but also from the students themselves.

Second, throughout the book we have argued for the need to value literacy not just in English but also in the mother tongue of language minorities. In keeping with this assumption, literacy programs should strive to promote both first and second language literacy in whatever way possible, given the constraints of cost and bilingual resources. Although programs will need to differ in design based on the local situation, they all should use the bilingual resources they have available to promote literacy in both languages. The reasons for doing so are many. First, as was pointed out in Chapter 1, there is increasing evidence that developing literacy in the mother tongue is beneficial to the development of second language literacy. Second, developing literacy in various languages will increase the literacy resources of the country, contributing both to the economic competitiveness of the country and to cross-cultural awareness. Third, and most important, promoting literacy in both the first and second language can minimize the potential negative effects on family life that occur when first language literacy is not validated outside of the family. Promoting mother tongue literacy can help to minimize the intergenerational conflicts illustrated in the previous chapter that are exacerbated by English-only school situations.

Finally, throughout the book we have illustrated the literacy demands that can exist in various contexts, be they amnesty tests or professional certification examinations. In order to help language minorities successfully meet these demands, literacy programs need to address the literacy demands set in the political, economic, and educational arenas. Which specific demands are included will, of course, depend on the needs of the learners. In many instances, however, literacy educators may need not only to help language minorities meet these requirements but also to work with their colleagues and students to change literacy requirements that are discriminatory on the basis of cultural background.

Literacy curricula

In addition to developing and implementing literacy programs that exhibit such characteristics, literacy educators need to develop curricula that meet the various literacy agendas of language minorities. For Minh, this might mean adopting a curriculum as technology orientation that deals with specialized medical skills and knowledge. For Maria, it might mean designing a curriculum that includes a common educational core orientation so that she will learn many of the academic skills her children are learning. It might also include a personal relevance orientation so that she can share her personal concerns regarding her family. For Melchora, it might mean designing a curriculum that includes a social adaptation orientation to teach specific job-related skills as well as a personal relevance orientation for her to deal with issues related to her family situation. In short, it will require that literacy educators be willing to adopt a variety of curriculum orientations rather than advocating one curriculum design for all.

Although the selection of the curriculum orientation will depend to a great extent on the needs of the learners, three principles should underlie the selection of the orientation, all of which develop from issues addressed in earlier chapters. First, we pointed out in Chapter 1 the danger of concluding that literacy is either a skill or a social practice. Rather, literacy includes skills used to engage in a range of social practices. In selecting a curriculum, literacy educators need to reject those that limit their focus exclusively to developing isolated skills. Instead, curricula need to give attention to both the discrete skills needed to deal with the printed word as well as to strategies that will enable students to use the printed word to extend knowledge and to solve intellectual, emotional, and social problems. Second, as was pointed out in Chapter 4, the content of the curriculum can be an important socializing agent. Because of this, curriculum content should be carefully selected to avoid any tendency to portray language minorities as belonging exclusively to a particular economic class or occupational role, thus suggesting that they have a limited role in the society.

Finally, throughout the book we have demonstrated how language minorities face a variety of conflicting literacy agendas that result from their role in their particular political, economic, educational, and family context. Whereas the political and educational structure may encourage an English-only literacy agenda, they may desire an agenda that includes mother-tongue literacy. Whereas their employers may want a literacy curriculum that focuses exclusively on job-related skills, they may have other literacy objectives. In order to address these conflicts, literacy curricula should draw on the social realities of the learners. Addressing such conflicts can provide opportunities for language minorities to share their concerns and consider options for resolving such conflicts.

Literacy assessment

In implementing such programs, literacy educators will also need to develop assessment measures that are appropriate to the specific program and curriculum. For Minh, assessment measures might include an evaluation of his ability to successfully complete exam items similar to those that will be on his professional certification test. It will also include, however, measures of progress that he himself considers important. Such assessment will occur throughout the program so that it can be used to direct the development of the course. For Carlos, assessment measures might include his drafting letters to union leaders, advocating changes in the workplace. Again, this would be ongoing throughout the program and include self-assessment measures. For Maria, assessment measures might include her teaching her children specific reading skills both in English and her native language as well as documenting any other measures of progress that she considers important.

In addition to developing a variety of assessment measures, literacy educators need to develop procedures for documenting progress in a manner that will be acceptable and comprehensible to the larger community. Unless they do this, the measures they design will be of little benefit in demonstrating the effectiveness of their literacy programs to the funding sources on which they depend. Literacy educators also need to work to convince funders that they are in the best position to know what constitutes progress since they are in daily contact with the learners.

When assessment is needed not to document progress but for gatekeeping purposes (such as to place students in classes or to sort those that qualify for professional certification), literacy educators need to convince test designers that literacy is a complex social practice that entails more than just isolated skills. In addition, literacy educators need to convince test designers that the inclusion of content that requires knowledge of a particular social class or cultural tradition unfairly penalizes those who do not share this tradition.

Literacy research

In successfully implementing such programs, literacy educators also need to undertake various kinds of research. They need to research the literacy needs of language minorities in their family, work, and community context so that better designed programs and curricula can be developed to meet the second language literacy agendas of language minorities. Literacy educators need to determine what purposes English literacy serves in the lives of language minorities and what other purposes these individuals would like it to serve. Literacy educators also need to examine what kinds of literacy programs exist in other communities and in other Anglophone countries for enabling language minorities to meet their literacy agendas, drawing on some of these ideas to develop innovative programs and curricula. Furthermore, they need to continue to research the process of becoming literate, particularly in reference to how first language literacy affects the acquisition of second language literacy. Finally, they need to research literacy practices as they exist in particular historical, economic, political, and cultural contexts so that they can better understand the second language literacy agendas of these contexts.

Literacy advocacy

In implementing such programs, literacy educators need to assume the role of advocate in both promoting institutional support and directing social attitudes. In terms of promoting institutional support, literacy educators need to work with private and public funders to convince them of the need for a variety of literacy programs and to suggest how the programs might be implemented. Moreover, literacy educators need to convince funders and elected officials that they share the responsibility to provide quality literacy programs. Unless literacy educators take these steps, they will not be able to provide the kind of literacy assistance their students desire. Lastly, literacy educators need to convince national leaders that if they wish an accurate account of the state of literacy in the nation, they must recognize that many language minorities are literate in their mother tongue. To miss this fact is to wrongly categorize a growing number of citizens as illiterate.

Most important, literacy educators need to promote social attitudes that see families such as the Trans, the Cierras, and the Galangs not as a problem with all of the stereotypes that this framework engenders, but as individuals who have specific second language literacy agendas, many of them set by forces beyond their control. By adopting this attitude in enacting second language literacy policies, political, business, and educational leaders hopefully will never lose sight of how their literacy policies are affecting individual lives.

References

Adult Literacy and Basic Skills Unit. (1989). *After the act: Developing basic skills work in the 1990s*. Educational Resource Information Center: Number 305 486.

Alderson, J. C. (1984). Reading in a foreign language: A reading problem or a language problem? In J. C. Alderson & A. H. Urquhart (Eds.), *Reading in a foreign language* (pp. 1–27). New York: Longman.

Anderson, R., & Pearson, D. (1988). A schema-theoretic view of basic processes in reading comprehension. In P. Carrell, J. Devine, & D. Eskey (Eds.), *Interactive approaches to second language reading* (pp. 37–55). New York: Cambridge University Press.

Apple, M. W. (1979). *Ideology and curriculum*. London: Routledge & Kegan Paul.

Aronowitz, S., & Giroux, H. (1988). Schooling, culture and literacy in the age of broken dreams: A review of Bloom and Hirsch. *Harvard Educational Review, 58*(2), 172–194.

Auerbach, E. (1986). Competency-based ESL: One step forward or two steps back? *TESOL Quarterly, 20*(3), 411–429.

Auerbach, E. (1989). Towards a social-contextual approach to family literacy. *Harvard Educational Review, 59*(2), 165–181.

Auerbach, E. (1990). *Making meaning, making change*. Boston, MA: University of Massachusetts English Family Literacy project.

Auerbach, E. (1991). Literacy and ideology. In W. Grabe (Ed.), *Annual Review of Applied Linguistics* (pp. 71–85). New York: Cambridge University Press.

Balliro, L. (1989). Reassessing assessment in adult ESL/literacy. Paper presented at the 22nd Annual TESOL Convention, San Antonio, Texas.

Bell, J., & Burnaby, G. (1984). *A handbook for ESL literacy*. Toronto, Canada: The Ontario Institute for Studies in Education.

Berlin, J. (1988). Rhetoric and ideology in the writing class. *College English, 50*(5), 477–494.

Burnaby, B. (1991). Adult literacy issues in Canada. In W. Grabe (Ed.), *Annual Review of Applied Linguistics* (pp. 156–171). Cambridge: Cambridge University Press.

California State Department of Education. (1982). *Vietnamese-speaking students*. University of California, Los Angeles: Evaluation, Dissemination and Assessment Center.

Canada Employment and Immigration Advisory Council. (1991). *Immigrants and language training*. Canada: Canada Employment and Immigration Advisory Council.

Canale, M., Frenette, N., & Belanger, M. (1988). Evaluation of minority student writing in first and second language. In J. Fine (Ed.), *Second language discourse: A textbook of current research*. Norwood, NJ: Ablex Publishing Corporation.

Carrell, P. (1988). Some causes of text-boundedness and schema interference in ESL reading. In P. Carrell, J. Devine, & D. Eskey (Eds.), *Interactive approaches to second language reading* (pp. 101–113). New York: Cambridge University Press.

Carrell, P., & Eisterhold, J. (1988). Schema theory and ESL reading pedagogy. In P. Carrell, J. Devine, & D. Eskey (Eds.), *Interactive approaches to second language reading* (pp. 73–92). New York: Cambridge University Press.

Carson, J., Carrell, P., Silberstein, S., Kroll, B., & Kuehn, P. (1990). Reading-writing relationships in first and second language. *TESOL Quarterly, 24*(2), 245–266.

Chall, J. S., & Snow, C. (1982). *Family and literacy: The contributions of out of school experiences to children's acquisition of literacy*. A final report to the National Institute of Education. Washington, DC: National Institute of Education.

Christie, F. (1990). The changing face of literacy. In F. Christie (Ed.), *Literacy for a changing world* (pp. 1–25). Victoria, Australia: The Australian Council for Educational Research.

Connor, U., & Kaplan, R. (Eds.). (1987). *Writing across languages: Analysis of L2 texts*. Reading, MA: Addison-Wesley.

Crandall, J. (1992). Adult literacy development. In W. Grabe (Ed.), *Annual Review of Applied Linguistics* (pp. 86–104). New York: Cambridge University Press.

Cumming, A. (1990). The thinking, interactions, and participation to foster in adult ESL literacy instruction. *TESL Talk, 20*(1), 34–51.

Cummins, J. (1981). The role of primary language development in promoting educational success for language minority students. In *Schooling and language minority students: A theoretical framework*. Los Angeles: Evaluation, Dissemination, and Assessment Center, California State University.

Cummins, J. (1982). *Mother tongue maintenance for minority language children: Some misconceptions*. Toronto, Canada: OISE Press.

Cummins, J. (1984). *Bilingualism and special education: Issues in assessment and pedagogy*. Clevedon, England: Multilingual Matters.

Delgado-Gaitan, C. (1987a). Mexican adult literacy: New directions for immigrants. In S. R. Goldman & H. T. Trueba (Eds.), *Becoming literate in English as a second language* (pp. 9–32). Norwood, NJ: Ablex Publishing Corporation.

Delgado-Gaitan, C. (1987b). Parent perceptions of school: Supportive environments for children. In T. Trueba (Ed.), *Success or failure? Learning and the language minority student* (pp. 131–155). New York: Newbury House.

Department of Education and Science (1975). *A language for life (The Bullock Report)*. London: Her Majesty's Stationery Office.

Department of Education and Science (1985). *Education for all: Report of the committee of inquiry into the education of children from ethnic minority groups (The Swann Report)*. London: Her Majesty's Stationery Office.

Department of Education and Science (1989). *Education for ages 5 to 16: Proposals of the Secretary of State for Education and Science and the Secretary of State for Wales (The Kingman Report)*. London: Her Majesty's Stationery Office.

Devall, S. (1987). Affirmative action and positive discrimination. In G. Haydon (Ed.), *Education for a pluralist society (Bedford Way Paper No. 30)* (pp. 85–93). London: University of London, Institute of Education.

Díaz, S., Moll, L., & Mehan, K. (1986). Socio-cultural resources in instruction: A context-specific approach. In California State Department of Education Bilingual Education Office, *Beyond language: Social and cultural factors in schooling language minority students* (pp. 187–230). Los Angeles: Evaluation, Dissemination, and Assessment Center, California State University.

Edwards, C., Moorhouse, J., & Widlake, S. (1988). Language or English? In J. Jones & A. West (Eds.), *Learning me your language: Perspectives on the teaching of English* (pp. 77–95). London: Mary Glasgow.

Fingeret, A. (1982). *The illiterate underclass: Demythologizing an American stigma*. Unpublished doctoral dissertation, Syracuse University, Syracuse, New York.

Fingeret, A. (1984). *Adult literacy education: current and future directions*. Washington, DC: ERIC Clearinghouse.

Fingeret, A. (1990). Literacy for what purpose: A response. In R. Venezky, D. Wagner, & B. Ciliberti (Eds.), *Toward defining literacy* (pp. 35–39). Newark, DE: International Reading Association.

Fisher, D. L. (1978). *Functional literacy and the school*. Washington, DC: National Institute of Education.

Foster, L., & Stockley, D. (1988). *Australian Multiculturalism: A documentary history and critique*. Philadelphia: Multilingual Matters.

Foucault, M. (1972). *The archaeology of knowledge.* New York: Vintage Books.

Freire, P. (1970). *Pedagogy of the oppressed.* New York: The Seabury Press.

Freire, P. (1974). *Education for critical consciousness.* New York: Continuum.

Gee, J. (1990). *Social linguistics and literacies: Ideology in discourses.* London: The Falmer Press.

Gee, J. (1991). Socio-cultural approaches to literacy (literacies). In W. Grabe (Ed.), *Annual Review of Applied Linguistics* (pp. 31–48). New York: Cambridge University Press.

Giroux, H. A. (1983). *Theory and resistance in education.* South Hadley, MA: Bergin and Garvey.

Goody, J. (1977). *The domestication of the savage mind.* Cambridge: Cambridge University Press.

Goody, J., & Watt, I. (1968). The consequences of literacy. In J. Goody (Ed.), *Literacy in traditional societies* (pp. 27–69). Cambridge: Cambridge University Press.

Gowen, S. (1990) *"Eyes on a different prize": A critical ethnography of a workplace literacy program.* Unpublished dissertation, Georgia State University, Atlanta, Georgia.

Grabe, W. (1988). Reassessing the term "interactive." In P. Carrell, J. Devine, & D. Eskey (Eds.), *Interactive approaches to second language reading* (pp. 36–70). New York: Cambridge University Press.

Graff, H. J. (1979). *The literacy myth: Literacy and social structure in the 19th century.* New York: Academic Press.

Habermas, J. (1987). *The theory of communicative action.* Boston: Beacon Press.

Hakuta, K. (1986). *Mirror of language: The debate on bilingualism.* New York: Basic Books.

Haverson, W. (1991). Adult literacy training. In M. Celce-Murcia (Ed.), *Teaching English as a second or foreign language* (pp. 185–194). New York: Newbury House.

Heath, S. B. (1980). The functions and uses of literacy. *Journal of Communication, 30,* 123–133.

Heath, S. B. (1983). *Ways with words: Language, life, and work in communities and classrooms.* Cambridge: Cambridge University Press.

Heath, S. B. (1986). Sociocultural contexts of language development. In California State Department of Education Bilingual Education Office, *Beyond language: Social and cultural factors in schooling language minority students* (pp. 143–186). Los Angeles: Evaluation, Dissemination, and Assessment Center, California State University.

Hinds, J. (1990). Inductive, deductive, quasi-inductive: Expository writing in Japanese, Korean, Chinese and Thai. In U. Connor & A. Johns (Eds.), *Coherence in writing* (pp. 87–110). Alexandria, VA: TESOL.

Hirsch, E. D. (1987). *Cultural literacy: What every American needs to know*. Boston: Houghton Mifflin.

Hogeland, C., & Rosen, K. (1990). *Dreams lost, dreams found: Undocumented women in the land of opportunity*. San Francisco: Coalition for Immigrant and Refugee Rights and Services, Immigrant Women's Task Force.

Holtzman, W. H., Diaz-Guerrero, R., & Swartz, J. D. (1975). *Personality development in two cultures: A cross-cultural longitudinal study of school children in Mexico and the United States*. Austin, TX: University of Texas Press.

Huebner, T. (1987). A socio-historical approach to literacy development: A comparative case study from the Pacific. In J. Langer (Ed.), *Language, literacy, and culture: Issues of society and schooling* (pp. 178–196). Norwood, NJ: Ablex Publishing Corporation.

Isserlis, J. (1991). Workplace literacy programs for nonnative English speakers. *ERIC Digest (October 1991)*.

Jensen, A. R. (1973). *Educability and group differences*. New York: Harper & Row.

Judd, E. (1987). The English language amendment: A case study on language and politics. *TESOL Quarterly, 21*(1), 113–135.

Kaestle, C. (1990). Policy implications of literacy definitions: A response. In R. Venezky, D. Wagner, & B. Ciliberti (Eds.), *Toward defining literacy* (pp. 63–69). Newark, DE: International Reading Association.

Kaplan, R. (1990). Introduction: Language planning in theory and practice. In R. Baldauf & A. Luke (Eds.), *Language planning and education in Australasia and the South Pacific* (pp. 3–13). Philadelphia: Multilingual Matters.

Khan, V. S. (1985). *Language education for all? Chapter 7 of the Swann Report*. London: University of London Institute of Education, Centre for Multicultural Education.

Kloss, J. (1971). The language rights of immigrant groups. *International Migration Review, 5*, 250–268.

Land, R. E., & Whitley, C. (1989). Evaluating second language essays in regular composition classes: Toward a pluralistic U.S. rhetoric. In D. Johnson & D. H. Roen (Eds.), *Richness in writing: Empowering ESL students* (pp. 284–293). New York: Longman.

Langer, J. (1987). A sociocognitive perspective on literacy. In J. Langer (Eds.), *Language, literacy and culture: Issues of society and schooling* (pp. 1–20). Norwood, NJ: Ablex Publishing Corporation.

Leibowitz, A. (1984). The official character of language in the United States: Literacy requirements for immigration, citizenship and entrance into American life. *Aztlan, 15*(1), 25–70.

Leichter, H. (1984). Families as environments for literacy. In H. Goelman, A. Oberg, & F. Smith (Eds.), *Awakening to literacy* (pp. 38–50). Portsmouth, NH: Heinemann Educational Books.

Levine, K. (1990). Contribution to the Forum: When a learner attempts to become literate in a second language, what is he or she attempting? *TESL Talk, 20*(1), 13–14.

lo Bianco, J. (1989). Foreword. In R. Wickert (Eds.), *No single measure. A survey of Australian adult literacy. Summary report.* Sydney, Australia: Institute of Technical and Adult Teacher Education, Sydney College of Advanced Education.

lo Bianco, J. (1990). Making language policy: Australia's experience. In R. Baldauf & A. Luke (Eds.), *Language planning and education in Australasia and the South Pacific* (pp. 47–79). Clevedon, England: Multilingual Matters.

Luke, A., McHoul, A. W., & Mey, J. L. (1990). On the limits of language planning: Class, state, and power. In R. B. Baldauf & A. Luke (Eds.), *Language planning and education in Australasia and the South Pacific* (pp. 25–46). Clevedon, England: Multilingual Matters.

Lytle, S., Belzer, A., Schultz, K., & Vannozzi, M. (1989). Learner-centered literacy assessment: An evolving process. In A. Fingeret & P. Jurmo (Eds.), *Participatory literacy education* (pp. 53–64). San Francisco: Jossey-Bass.

Lytle, S., & Wolfe, M. (1989). *Adult literacy education: Program evaluation and learner assessment.* Columbus, OH: ERIC Clearinghouse on Adult, Career, and Vocational Education.

Lytle, S. L. (1988). From inside out: Reinventing assessment. *Focus on Basics, 2*(1).

Macias, R. (1990a). Bilingualism, multilingualism and multiculturalism. In W. Grabe & R. Kaplan (Eds.), *Introduction to applied linguistics* (pp. 211–228). Reading, MA: Addison-Wesley.

Macias, R. (1990b). Definitions of literacy: A response. In R. Venezky, D. Wagner, & B. Ciliberti (Eds.), *Toward defining literacy* (pp. 17–22). Newark, DE: International Reading Association.

Martin-Jones, M. (1989). Language education in the context of linguistic diversity: Differing orientations in educational policy. In J. H. Esling (Ed.), *Multicultural education and policy: ESL in the 1990s* (pp. 36–58). Toronto, Canada: OISE Press.

Mikulecky, L. (1990). Literacy for what purpose. In R. Venezky, D. Wagner, & B. Ciliberti (Eds.), *Toward defining literacy* (pp. 24–34). Newark, DE: International Reading Association.

Morey, B. E. (1989). *Review of adult literacy activities: A commonwealth perspective.* ERIC Document 315–626.

National Council for Mother Tongue Teaching (1985). The Swann Report: Education for all? *Journal of Multilingual and Multicultural Development, 6*(6), 497–508.

Norment, N. (1986). Organizational structure of Chinese subjects writing in Chinese and in ESL. *Journal of the Chinese Language Teachers Association, 23,* 49–72.

Ogbu, J., & Matute-Bianchi, M. E. (1986). Understanding sociocultural factors: knowledge, identity, and school adjustment. In California State Department of Education Bilingual Education Office, *Beyond language: Social and cultural factors in schooling language minority students* (pp. 72–142). Los Angeles: Evaluation, Dissemination, and Assessment Center, California State University.

Olson, D. (1977). From utterance to text: the bias of language in speech and writing. *Harvard Educational Review, 47*(3).

Olson, D. (1990). Contribution to the Forum: When a learner attempts to become literate in a second language, what is he or she attempting? *TESL Talk, 20*(1), 18–20.

Ong, W. J. (1982). *Orality and literacy: The technologizing of the word.* London: Methuen.

Osterloh, K. (1986). Intercultural differences and communicative approaches to foreign language teaching in the third world. In J. Valdes (Ed.), *Culture bound* (pp. 77–84). New York: Cambridge University Press.

Otheguy, R., & Otto, R. (1980). The myth of static maintenance in bilingual education. *Modern Language Journal, 64*(3), 350–355.

Paulston, C. B. (1980). *Bilingual education: Theories and issues.* Rowley, MA: Newbury House.

Phillipson, R. (1992). *Linguistic imperialism.* Oxford: Oxford University Press.

Rangel, E. (1990). English family literacy programs: Building on the resources of the home. *ERIC/CLL New Bulletin, 14*(1), 6–8.

Read, C., & Mackay, R. (1984). *Illiteracy among adult immigrants in Canada.* Educational Resource Information Center: Number 291 875.

Reder, M. (1987). Comparative aspects of functional literacy development: Three ethnic American communities. In D. A. Wagner (Ed.), *The future of literacy in a changing world* (pp. 250–269). Oxford: Pergamon Press.

Reid, E. (1988). Linguistic minorities and language education – The English experience. *Journal of Multilingual and Multicultural Development, 6*(6), 181–191.

Richmond, J. (1992). Literacy and learning in a national curriculum: Significant developments in the teaching of literacy in Britain over the last 15 years. Paper presented at University of California, Berkeley, seminar series of the National Center for the Study of Writing and Literacy.

Rotberg, I. (1984). Bilingual education policy in the United States. *Prospectus, 14*(1), 133–147.

Sarmiento, A., & Kay, A. (1990). *Worker-centered learning: A union guide to workplace literacy.* Washington DC: AFL-CIO Human Resources Development Institute.

Schieffelin, B., & Cochran-Smith, M. (1984). Learning to read culturally: Literacy before schooling. In H. Goelman, A. Oberg, & F. Smith (Eds.), *Awakening to literacy* (pp. 3–23). Portsmouth, NH: Heinemann Educational Books.

Scribner, S., & Cole, M. (1981). *The psychology of literacy.* Cambridge, MA: Harvard University Press.

Shaw, J. M., & Dowsett, G. W. (1986). *The evaluation process in the adult migrant education program.* Adelaide, Australia: National Curriculum Resource Centre Adult Migrant Education Program, Australia.

Skutnabb-Kangas, T. (1981). Guest worker or immigrant: Different ways of reproducing an underclass. *Journal of Multilingual and Multicultural Development, 2,* 89–113.

Spener, D. (1988). Transitional bilingual education and the socialization of immigrants. *Harvard Educational Review, 58*(2), 133–153.

Stasiulis, D. (1990). *Multiculturalism and the economic agenda in Australia: Adult ESL, overseas skills recognition and anti-racist strategies.* Canada: Policy and Research, Multiculturalism Sector, Multiculturalism and Citizenship.

Street, B. (1984). *Literacy in theory and practice.* Cambridge: Cambridge University Press.

Street, B. (1991). Cross-cultural literacy. Paper presented at Conference on Intergenerational Literacy, Teachers' College, Columbia University.

Stuckey (1991). *The violence of literacy.* Portsmouth, NH: Boyton/Cook Publishers.

Sue, S., & Padilla, A. (1986). Ethnic minority issues in the United States: Challenges for the educational system. In California State Department of Education Bilingual Education Office, *Beyond language: Social and cultural factors in schooling language minority students* (pp. 35–72). Los Angeles: Evaluation, Dissemination, and Assessment Center, California State University.

Therborn, G. (1980). *The ideology of power and the power of ideology.* London: Verso.

Thompson, G., & Martin, P. L. (1991). Immigration reform and the agricultural labor force. *Labor Law Journal, 42*(8), 528–535.

Tollefson, J. W. (1991). *Planning language, planning inequality.* New York: Longman.

Torruellas, R., Benmayer, R., Goris, A., & Juarbe, A. (1991). Affirming cultural citizenship in the Puerto Rican community: Critical literacy and the El Barrio popular education program. In C. Walsh (Ed.), *Literacy as praxis* (pp. 183–221). Norwood, NJ: Ablex Publishing Corporation.

Trueba, H. (1984). The forms, functions, and values of literacy: Reading for survival in a barrio as a student. *NABE Journal, 9*(1), 21–39.

Trueba, H. (1989). *Raising silent voices: Educating the linguistic minorities for the 21st century.* New York: Newbury House.

Venezky, R. (1990). Definitions of literacy. In R. Venezky, D. Wagner, & B. Ciliberti (Eds.), *Toward defining literacy* (pp. 2–16). Newark, DE: International Reading Association.

Wallace, C. (1988). *Learning to read in a multicultural society: The social context of second language literacy.* London: Prentice-Hall.

Walsh, C. (1991). Literacy as praxis: A framework and an introduction. In C. Walsh (Ed.), *Literacy as praxis* (pp. 1–24). Norwood, NJ: Ablex Publishing Corporation.

Weinstein, G. (1984). Literacy and second language acquisition: Issues and perspectives. *TESOL Quarterly, 18*(3), 471–484.

Weinstein-Shr, G. (1990). Family and intergenerational literacy in multilingual families. *Center for Applied Linguistics National Clearinghouse on Literacy Education* (August 1990), 1–4.

Weinstein-Shr, G. (in press). Adult Biliteracy in the United States. In D. Spener (Ed.), *Bi-literacy.* Washington DC: Center for Applied Linguistics and Delta Systems Company.

Wells, B. (1987). Apprenticeship in literacy. *Interchange, 18*(1–2), 109–123.

Wickert, R. (1989). *No single measure. A survey of Australian adult literacy.* Sydney, Australia: Institute of Technical and Adult Teacher Education, Sydney College of Advanced Education.

Wiley, T. (1991). Measuring the nation's literacy: Important considerations. *ERIC Digest* (July 1991).

Williams, J., & Snipper, G. (1990). *Literacy and bilingualism.* New York: Longman.

Wong Fillmore, L. (1991). When learning a second language means losing the first. *Early Childhood Research Quarterly, 6,* 323–346.

Wrigley, H. (1988). *Tell me the name of Grant's horse: Language issues in the 1986 Immigration Act, March 1988.* Tomás Rivera Center: Tomás Rivera Center Working Paper. California State University, Long Beach.

Wrigley, H. (1989). *One hundred questions. The ongoing debate over language issues in the 1986 Immigration Act, part 2,.* Tomás Rivera Center: Tomás Rivera Center Working Paper. California State University, Long Beach.

Wrigley, H. (1991). National English literacy demonstration program for adults of limited English proficiency. Paper presented at the Language Minority Literacy Workshop, University of California at Santa Barbara.

Wrigley, H., & Guth, G. (1992). *Bringing literacy to life: Issues and options in adult ESL literacy.* San Mateo, CA: Aguirre International.

Index